THE LIFE

OF

JAMES McCURREY.

JAMES McCURREY.

THE LIFE
OF
JAMES McCURREY
(FROM 1801 TO 1876),

CONTAINING

THIRTY-NINE YEARS' EXPERIENCE
AS A TEMPERANCE ADVOCATE AND MISSIONARY,
COLLATED FROM HIS PERSONAL NARRATIVE,
JOURNALS, &c.

"Out of the depths have I cried unto Thee, O Lord."—*Ps.* cxxx. 1.
"He brought me up also out of an horrible pit, out of the miry clay, and set my feet upon a rock, and established my goings."—*Ps.* xl. 2.

London:

S. W. PARTRIDGE & CO., 9, PATERNOSTER ROW.

TO THE

Memory of my beloved Wife

MARGARET McCURREY,

I INSCRIBE THIS RECORD OF MY LIFE,

AS A SMALL TRIBUTE OF GRATITUDE FOR THE PATIENCE

WITH WHICH SHE BORE WITH ME

FOR MANY YEARS,

AND THE HELP SHE RENDERED ME TO OVERCOME

MY BESETTING SIN OF INTEMPERANCE,

AND ASSISTED ME IN MY EFFORTS TO RESCUE OTHERS

FROM THAT VICE,

AND RESTORE THEM TO THE PATHS OF

SOBRIETY AND RELIGION.

CONTENTS.

CHAPTER I.
Introductory.—Early Life 9

CHAPTER II.
Comes to London.—Drink in the Household and its Consequences.—A Mystery.—Conversion.—Relapse.—The Pledge.—Deliverances 18

CHAPTER III.
A New Career.—After Signing the Pledge.—Trials, Temptations, and Persecutions 33

CHAPTER IV.
Records of my Children 42

CHAPTER V.
Open-air Advocacy.—Its Commencement in Chelsea.—Public-house Corners.—"White Stiles."—Itinerating in Westminster, Seven Dials.—Drunken People.—Summary of Work 48

CHAPTER VI.
First Steps towards Independence in Worldly Circumstances.—Sabbath Convictions. 72

CONTENTS.

CHAPTER VII.

Sad Records of the Victims—Warnings 81

CHAPTER VIII.

Brief Records of the Rescued 118

CHAPTER IX.

The Case of Matthews.—Miscellaneous Records and Notes of Experience 133

CHAPTER X.

Missionary Work in Different Places. 151

CHAPTER XI.

Recognition of Services to the Cause.—Recollections of Fellow-Workers in the Early Days of the Movement 171

CHAPTER XII.

Recollections of Father Mathew and of Special Occasions . . 179

CHAPTER XIII.

Loss of the Companion of my Life 182

CHAPTER XIV.

Conclusion.—The Evening of Life 189

THE LIFE

OF

JAMES McCURREY

(FROM 1801 TO 1876).

CHAPTER I.

INTRODUCTORY.—EARLY LIFE.

IF any apology were needed in presenting this simple, and I trust faithful, record of my life, I may say that I have been so often urged by my temperance friends to give it to the public that I grow weary of apologizing for not complying with their wishes. Moreover, such of my personal and relative experiences as I have given at public meetings and elsewhere have been considered useful, both in building up converts to sobriety, and in warning and rescuing many whose feet were slipping from the inclined plane of moderation, and also those who had fallen into the quagmire of intemperance.

My aim, I trust—my single aim, whether in speaking or writing—has only been to do good. I have no personal desire for notoriety, still less for self-glorification; indeed, I am deeply conscious that I need to humble myself constantly before God, and ever to bless the Divine grace and mercy that sought me when I wandered, preserved me from utter ruin when I fell, lifted me from outer darkness into His marvellous light, and filled my soul with an earnest longing to seek and succour those who, like myself, were slaves to sin and Satan through intemperance. If "each man's life is all men's lesson," my life presents the record of such a sinner saved that none need despair, and of humble efforts to do good so owned and blessed that all may emulate. It has pleased my Heavenly Father, amid what has been a successful career, yet to try me with many and varied afflictions, and still to sustain me, so that when I have had to mourn the loss of all my immediate descendants, my Saviour's love has been with me, and I may thankfully and in lowly reverence take the words of the Apostle, and say, "Troubled on every side, yet not distressed; we are perplexed, but not in despair; persecuted, but not forsaken; cast down, but not destroyed." 2 Cor. iv. 8, 9.

I was born in Glasgow, May 18, 1801. My parents, both natives of Scotland, and by long descent on both sides of Scottish lineage, were industrious, worthy people; one of those households which, I think, are more frequently found north than south of the Tweed: strong in health, full of energy, and gifted, some of them, with unusually good abilities. I often recall the home of my childhood, and see, as the central figure around whom all tenderly gathered, my dear, good mother. She was a woman of a loving spirit, sound judgment, and humble piety: not a loud professor, but possessing the real heartfelt influence of love to God, which made her a blessing to her husband and children—a blessing, I grieve to say, not enough valued.

The family consisted of one daughter, Jane, and three sons, Andrew, John, and James (myself); I was the youngest. My father was a carpenter, but as it was then the war time, he had so great a demand for packing-cases and trunks that his business was chiefly in that department of wood-work.

My eldest brother Andrew was early in life noted as a very skilful workman, and became a violin-maker of great repute, and earned such high wages as a workman, even before he set up for himself, that he might have easily become a wealthy man. My brother John did not like his father's occupation, and gave up the carpenter's bench for the trade of a bricklayer, mason, and builder. He also, from his great strength, clear head, and quick hand, was a first-rate workman.

I was big of my age, full of fun and frolic, and not very fond of school, or easy to keep out of mischief. I remember now my mother's prayers, and how she taught me out of the "Shorter Catechism," and tried to fill my mind with texts of Scripture and simple hymns and psalms. I know that I did not attend. I was more wild and giddy than children generally are, for I was full of strong life, high spirits, and resolute self-will; but yet words I little heeded at that time, or openly disobeyed, took hold of me somehow. They were seed that, falling into a stiff, rank soil and choked with weeds, still did not all die. Poor dear mother! she did indeed cast her bread upon the waters, and it has been found after many days. Of all the recollections of my childhood none are so vivid as her sorrow at my waywardness and her prayers. My father paid a guinea a quarter for my schooling, but I was a truant; used to swim all the summer, and slide all the winter, instead of going to school. The reader may say, "But why did not your father control you, and compel you to go to school? Why were you, when in a prosperous household among skilful workmen, obliged, at the early age of ten or eleven, when you should have been at school, to go into the workshop?" The answer is not far to seek. My father had many good qualities, but sobriety was not among them.

I have said it was war time; work was plentiful, and wages high. All these things were incentives to whisky drinking. The customs of society among all classes encouraged drinking. The man who could take the most strong drink without being overcome by it was considered the most sober man. As to any one doing without intoxicating drink, it was never thought of. At births, marriages, funerals, apprenticeships, there were established drinking customs, which it was considered disgraceful to evade; while in workshops, drink fines and footings were the arbitrary rule. My chief employment when first I went into my father's workshop was (being the youngest) to fetch the drink in for the men, and my reward to have a "sup for mysel'."

Of an evening the public-houses would be full of working men hearing and discussing the war news from abroad, or the bitter party politics at home—all of them thirsty subjects; and I need not say that, high as the wages were, the homes were mostly none the better for them. My dear mother never gave any sanction by her own habits to this rage for strong drink. I never saw her touch spirits, or anything but a half-pint of warm beer now and then, which I suppose in that time she might think she could not do without. Indeed her toils were great and her comforts few; for though my father was a quiet man in his drink and very fond of her, he had a foolish, maudlin way of speaking to his dear "Annie" when he had been drinking, which, while it caused laughter to us boys, was a great vexation to our mother. She knew, and, on reflection, I too are convinced, that he lost his influence over us children. A man either becomes tyrannical or foolish in his family when he yields to strong drink. In either case a cruel wrong is done, for the children lose their love and respect. All just rule is at an end, and the wilfulness of youth is unchecked.

So it came to pass that we boys did pretty much as we liked in over-hours. We worked hard in the workshop, and we worked with equal energy in the devil's workshop—the public-house. Our very health and strength—God's good gifts—were perverted to evil. As I look back, I am lost in wonder at the infinite mercy of God that He did not utterly leave Himself without a witness in my wayward spirit. I loved my mother, and pitied her. I did not imitate her, but her example kept up some faint belief in my mind that there was a something real and lovely in piety and prayer, though I did not try them for myself.

It is the character of sin and folly to make people dissatisfied and restless. I was tired of working for my father; and as my brother John had gone to the building trade, I resolved to go to that also; and also as my mother may have thought it better that I should no longer work at my father's trade I was not opposed in my wish, and so I commenced my apprenticeship as a bricklayer. I can certainly say that never in all my early years did I ever hear any warnings against strong drink, any censure of the public-house, or any great condemnation of drunkenness, unless it led to some breach of the law or loss of life, when such excuses would be used as "Poor fellow! he was soon overcome;" "He was no one's enemy but his own," &c.

Need I say that my restlessness did not leave me when I left my father's workshop. Once I set off to Paisley, and being primed with drink, and fired by the bands playing, and the colours flying of a marching regiment that passed through, I resolved to enlist. By some means my mother heard that I had spoken of some such intention, and she came to Paisley seeking her wanderer with tears, and implored me, as I was her youngest, not to leave her. Some vague wonder must have filled my mind that she should love me after all I had done to vex and trouble her. I did not think then, but I have often thought since, that a mother's love is a reflection from the Sun and Source of all love. Jesus seeks the wanderer from the fold. When the prodigal is yet afar off He sees him, and as soon as the feeblest step is taken back from the paths of sin runs to meet and restore him.

I cannot reproach myself with not having some feeling for my mother. I saw that my father's drinking made her life sad; that Andrew, with all his ample earnings, was not a comfort to her; that John, a fine, kind-hearted young man, was too much "a good fellow" among his companions to be good at home. I saw their faults, and it may be resented them, but I did not restrain myself any the more.

Among my father's intimate friends was a very clever mechanic, named Clark. This man and my father had known each other well in boyhood. They were neighbours for years; then they separated, Mr. Clark having married and settled some distance from Glasgow. When I was about the age of sixteen, the intimacy of early years was renewed between Clark and my father, and their friendship might have been in all ways a source of good, but that it was cemented by that which poisons all wholesome intercourse, strong drink. Plenty of means—the result of remarkable skill in the finest art of instrument making—led of course to plenty of drinking. There was a family, and I became as intimate with the young people as my father was with the head of the house; an intimacy I recall with an interest that can never cease to be dear and precious to me, because of the influence it had in one important particular in my future career.

Mrs. Clark, the mother, took rather to me, and was often praising me. My own dear mother was placed at the disadvantage of being the only one in our family who, speaking freely, while tenderly, told me of my faults. I often felt that I was hardly dealt by, when she was doing me the greatest kindness a mother can do; and I, therefore, was open to the temptation of being praised rather than warned by a woman who was also a mother of a large family, and who had no special dislike to the drinking customs of the time, or deep feeling of the sin and sorrow that they led to. I often used then to contrast her leniency with my mother's strictness, especially on one subject. Mrs. Clark frequently named an absent daughter, "a braw lassie—Maggie," and I felt soon a great curiosity, which I would not own, to see this girl. She was learning the business of a dressmaker at a neighbouring town, and soon after I grew intimate in the Clark family she paid her home a visit. I had an awkward shyness of, and rather distrusted or felt a kind of contempt for, girls. " I don't want to hear about their Maggie," I said to myself; but it came to pass that I met her first on the stairs, and I must have been very much struck with her, for I recollect it as if her likeness was photographed on my mind from that hour. It was a very important visit to me, for, great rough youth as I was, I felt that life would be utterly worthless to me unless shared with her.

Those who know me know that my nature is not quiet or calm. Until the grace of God spoke peace to my turbulent spirit, I was in constant danger from the impetuosity of my feelings, and on looking back to what I was when I ventured to look up to my sweet Margaret, I am amazed that so good and sensible a girl noticed me. But so it was. Our love was mutual, and as pure, humanly speaking, as it was strong and enduring.

It was a comfort to me that my mother too liked Margaret.

I had a strong if secret opinion that my mother's judgment was sound, and I had feared that as I was very young she would either oppose my inclination in this matter, or make a joke of my affection, as most other members of both families did. But that trial I had not to endure from her.

About this time, 1818, the Clark family removed to London. Mr. Clark's great mechanical skill was recognized, and very good prospects opened for him and his sons. However, as their going was only an experiment which might not succeed, they did not oppose their daughter Margaret remaining with friends in Glasgow. Of course, the kindness of my mother made our house the frequent resort of Margaret, and though I was but a lad in years I looked far older than my age; older than Margaret, who was my senior. I had all my boyhood up tried to be manly in many foolish and bad things, as smoking, drinking, and spending my money and time in tavern sports and associations; but, amid all, so much of truer manliness remained that I was reckoned a good and very expeditious workman, always employed on any difficult or special job; but I was not out of my time, and my wages were only nine shillings a week. Nevertheless, my Maggie consented to take me "for better for worse"—ah! for many a long year it was worse, before the better time came. The Rev. H. Muschat married us in my father's house among our assembled friends, as is the custom in Scotland, on November 19, 1819. I well remember an incident at the wedding; the rev. gentleman was troubled with a cough, and of course found it needful to have some remedy, and therefore took a copious drink of whisky; which, either going the wrong way, or suddenly irritating his throat, threw him into such a state that he seemed choking, and pronounced us man and wife with the utmost difficulty, as he was panting for breath and almost black in the face. My young wife, who had no great favour for whisky, and never touched it, used to say it had nearly broken off our marriage ceremony, and we recalled it often in after years as a very significant fact on our wedding-day.

Some may say facts do not bear out my praise of Margaret as a sensible lass; that nothing could be more imprudent than her taking a wild slip of a lad not nineteen as a husband, with nine shillings a week to keep house on; but love "laughs at impossibilities, and cries, it shall be done."

There was some good sense in the way my young wife set about making our home, poor as it was, a place of comfort, and working at her own business to help the household stock. My mother sent us a chest of drawers, and some other household furniture, and my brother Andrew gave us a waggon of coals; but, after all, it was hard times with us that first winter. Thanks to my wife's good influence I left off going to the public-house, and thought something of how the private house at home was to be kept. Good work at my wife's business was slow in coming in, but Margaret was the last woman in the world to sit idle, because she could not get the exact work she had been used to. She got umbrella covers to run together, and the pay being very small I used of an evening to thread scores of needles ready for her use, that she might have no interruption in her ill-paid toil. It was something new to see me sitting at home of a night threading needles after my rough work during the day, and it seems to me now as unreal as a dream. Yet I am glad to remember it, for I know it must have comforted my dear wife amid her many early trials, that however poor our lot we were rich in love. And my deliberate opinion is, after more than fifty years from that needle-threading time, that the best treasure in a poor man's house, or a rich man's either, is faithful love.

CHAPTER II.

COMES TO LONDON.—DRINK IN THE HOUSEHOLD AND ITS CONSEQUENCES.—A MYSTERY.—CONVERSION.—RELAPSE.—THE PLEDGE.—DELIVERANCES.

WHILE we were struggling on in our first year of married life, my wife heard of the prosperity of her father and brothers in London. It was natural for her to wish me to be better off as I became out of my time, and the winter being come, and our first child born, made us both inclined to look to the south. I can safely say that in resolving to leave the home of my youth, I not only wished to benefit myself and my wife, but I had the strong desire to help my mother; for as my poor father's habits were no better, but went on at the usual rate of low society until they were reaching the lowest, there was a constant sorrow sitting at the old fireside. So we resolved to mend a bad matter by trying new scenes, and in 1821 we came to London. One circumstance of our departure from Glasgow gives a keen pang to my heart even now. There had been some opposition on the part of my family to our removal, and as is often the case in family disputes we all grew warm, and my parents said many things they did not mean; and as my father's drinking had been one main cause of my yielding to my wife's wish to join her people in London, I was not slow to give angry replies. I suppose in the strife we were all wrong. I know I was, for my passions were too fierce for any restraint but religion, and that I had not then. Maggie, ever a peace-maker, tried to mediate so that we might part friendly, but I was obstinate. I well remember that on the day we went away my wife had taken an affectionate leave of my poor mother, for the attachment between them was great on both sides, while I stood out in the street and would not go in. When my wife found me and we walked away, my mother ran after us up the street, calling me back to kiss her; and in my stubborn rage I would not return. I waved my hand and went on, her voice ringing in my ear, " Jamie, lad, come back a wee !" Oh ! that I had gone, and had that last kiss, it would have been a precious memory to me now.

We were very kindly received by Mr. and Mrs. Clark, my wife's father and mother.

I have spoken of the great mechanical skill of my wife's father, and he was now prospering greatly as a dentist. It was not then by any means so frequently practised as now, and very costly prices were paid for all the mechanical appliances of dental surgery. He lived in a good house in Maddox-street, Bond-street, had plenty of work, and earned a large income. Compared with the sums I had been used to in Glasgow, it seemed to us as if they were in the way of making a fortune easily. But young as I was, I might soon have known that it is not what men earn but what they spend, which must be reckoned before real prosperity can be attained. My wife had the good sense to see this, and dread the waste and drinking in her father's house.

Very soon she wished that we had a home of our own, however humble; she hated intemperance, though then she did not see the way clearly out of it. I got work at my trade, and was a little subject to jeers among my fellow-workmen for my north-country speech. They mostly called me

"Scottie," but the master soon noticed that if quickness and strength were wanted, Scottie was the man. Ah, and Scottie was the man for a song and a spree; and the habit of taking sips from boyhood laid the foundation of deep drinking in manhood.

When a man is dissatisfied with himself he is sure to be restless for some change in his outward condition. Death and life had both come to our dwelling in our first two years in London. Our first babe died in infancy, and in a year after another was sent to comfort the poor mother, and to make the house more homely. Well, I did not settle. I dearly loved my wife and child, but drink came between me and them. Ever on my senses returning, my remorse was horrible—more than I could bear; I longed to get away from my work, from London, anywhere. It was just at this time that I received, through the Clark family, tidings that my mother was ill. All my early tenderness revived, and I flew to my wife and told her. We had no money saved, good as my wages were. Mr. Clark would not lend me money, for he seldom had any to spare—certainly not, to help me to go away from my work; but my Maggie understood the strong feeling of my heart and shared it. "We will go," she said, "at any sacrifice;" and so we sold off all our little stock of household goods, and set off at once to Scotland, my mother's voice, "Jamie, come back!" seeming to sound in my ears. Judge what my feelings were, when after a toilsome journey, my wife and child worn and exhausted, for travelling was hard work in those days, I stood once more within the doors of my early home.

My mother was not there; she had gone to her heavenly home! I was nearly mad with grief, and soon also with rage. A woman came to meet us who had evidently been drinking. I say nothing of my father; I do not like to recall the scene, but I am pledged to denounce drink as the cause of domestic misery. This nurse or housekeeper, blazing with drink, sitting in my mother's place, roused my passions so much that what with grief and rage I was frenzied, and it was through the infinite mercy of God that I did not do some desperate deed.

My brother John, now a prosperous, married man, but none the less a slave to strong drink, dragged me away, and we mourned in an enraged, desperate way together.

We set off to the cemetery where my mother was buried, and found the gates closed for the night; but nothing could keep me from her grave. We scaled the gates, and there, on her last resting-place, I laid me down ready to die with agony that I had refused her last kiss, flung away from her in anger, made no return for all her love and sorrow. Indeed the sorrows of her life seemed to rise to my recollection only to add to my utter misery. Yet, amid all the pangs of grief, it never entered my head that drink had ruined her home, and that I ought to be rid of its snares.

All was so changed to me in Glasgow that my wife urged me to bring my visit to a close and return to London. My brother Andrew was living in very good circumstances as to worldly matters with his wife and family, but he was, or seemed to us, proud and cold. He thought his position gave him authority to condemn my father, and to lecture John and me; but knowing he drank as much as the rest—and, indeed, never left off the habit, and was ultimately ruined by it—we were not willing to bear his censures; so I felt I had lost not only my mother, but was cut adrift from my father and brother, and the sooner I retraced my way to the south the better.

We returned in a poor plight, and I went to work at once, and with my wife's economy we managed to gather another little home about us. One result of this visit north, and my conversation with my brother John in Glasgow, was that in about two or it may be three years, after having long, it seems, in a restless way talked about it, he suddenly started off for London, resolving to seek work in the metropolis. He was to send for his wife and family if he succeeded; if not, he was to return home.

Of course his first job was to find me, our circumstances having been but poor after that sad journey to Scotland. We had not kept up much intercourse with the Clarks; indeed, rather hid our place of residence from them, merely calling now and then on my wife's parents and brothers; so John did not know my address, for we wrote but seldom, and, like the London workman, I shifted my lodgings frequently, to be near my work, which then was often changing.

My poor brother was very persevering. He went to every new building he saw, inquiring for a young Scotchman. Regent-street was building then, and I was employed there. My name, Scottie, stuck to me; and when the men heard my brother inquiring, they told him there was a man of the north called Scottie, and one came and called me to him. Judge of my joy when I saw my favourite brother, and heard the old familiar speech of my childhood.

Oh! it was a joyful meeting. Why cannot I recall it with joy? Why is it that so many scenes of my life are painful in the retrospect? Reader, at the risk of being wearisome, it is the truth, strong drink marred all.

Off we went, my brother and I, to have a carouse at meeting. We both drank deep. My brother did tell me where he lodged, I think, but I am not clear. I can remember that he refused to go home with me, and I may have seen he was not fit to go just then and see my wife. I was ready enough to keep her from being troubled with other people in their cups, if I did not read myself the same lessons. Suffice it, we parted somewhere near where the Regent Circus, Piccadilly, was then building. From that hour I never saw my brother John, or could find out what became of him! I made fruitless inquiries at hospitals, police stations, and workhouses. His wife, poor thing, distracted about him, did all she could, but not a trace of him was ever found. Lost in the great ocean of London, dropped out of life in the early prime of his days, his fate, in its woful mystery, haunted me for years, and was, I grieve to say, in the early time of my sorrow, a frequent excuse for drinking and for haunting drinking places, only to learn that such mysterious losses of friends were far more frequent than those unacquainted with the drinking customs in the lower stratum of life would think possible.

There was no new police then, and the press was not such a power as it now is. The dark places of the capital were left in their darkness.

MY CONVERSION.

Some hard times followed our sad loss; years of trial to my wife, of reproach to me, in which I was miserable when drunk and more miserable when sober, when occurred the most memorable event of my life. This was undoubtedly my conversion to God, in the year 1828-9. Many persons may think *the* most memorable event was my signing the pledge, but as eternity is superior to time, so is a man's eternal salvation to his temporal salvation. Had it not been for the pledge, however, it is very clear to my mind that I could not have maintained my Christian standing. My conversion occurred subsequently to a conversation with a Mr. Ponsford. I went to work in Theobald's Road, Holborn, for a very respectable master builder, and I remained with him about two years. The religious convictions which led to this result occurred at the very time I was in the act of persecuting a very good and pious man with whom I was associated in the building work which was done there. Great was the persecution this stout-hearted fellow endured from those about him. They called him by all the names they could think of that were bad. There were two men who made themselves particularly conspicuous in their persecution of the man whom afterwards I was proud to call my friend. They were working in a gentleman's house in the neighbourhood of the Foundling Hospital, and having secured and primed themselves with a bottle of his rum, they were ready for what they called "a lark," and so was I, for I joined them. I went downstairs to where the man of prayer was, with the intention of beginning to curse and to swear, but I could not open my mouth. I stood a moment or two, and then left the spot.

"Why, Scottie"—a nickname they had for me—"you never said a word to him."

For a moment I could not answer the speaker. "I don't want to have anything at all to do with him."

That was not the end of it. My conscience troubled me. My past life rose up like a black cloud against me, and seemed to frown upon me. I walked about as one in a terrible dream, who would awake shortly to a still more terrible reality. The past was full of terror, and in the future there seemed to be no hope. I went to the man whom I had attempted to insult. It was a bright afternoon, and the sun streamed through the windows of the house where he was working. I said,—

" It's a beautiful afternoon, Mr. Withers."

"Yes," he said, " it is."

" How brightly the sun shines!"

"Oh! Mr. McCurrey," he said, "if the Sun of Righteousness was to shine as brilliantly upon your soul as the sun of the firmament does, what a happy and what a useful man you might be!"

Merciful me! Instead of getting the help I expected from him, I only seemed to be thrown back deeper and deeper. At last I asked him what was the place of worship he attended, for, I added, "I should like to go to it."

He at once said, "I will call for you."

I declined his offer, but went alone to Great Queen-street chapel, and heard a sermon by the Rev. John Anderson:—"I forgave thee all that debt, because thou desiredst me: shouldest not thou also have had compassion on thy fellowservant, even as I had pity on thee?" (Matt. xviii. 32, 33). This roused me to a sense both of God's mercy in Christ, and of my duty to fellow-sinners. It was a new and guiding light to my soul. When I went home I was pleased to think that there was hope for me, but I could not yet understand that it was by believing in Christ. I spoke to ministers on the subject, but that seemed to be a blank to me; still I went to the chapel again, and again, and again. On one occasion I remember going into a coal cellar, and kneeling among the coals, where I prayed God to grant me His mercy. On another occasion I went into the vaults of a house where I was working, and wrestled with God in prayer. I was this time startled by a man giving a sudden knock at the door and entering.

"Why," he said, "you've been praying."

"Me praying! what are you talking about?"

"Why," he said, "I could hear you praying."

I denied it vehemently, as Peter did before me, and then was ashamed of my conduct even as Peter also had been. I went from the vaults to the top of the house, and stood there looking over the parapet. An awful sensation came over me. The sensation was this, that if I threw myself over I should not be killed, but I would be taken to the hospital, where a minister or ministers would see me, and then I should find out the way whereby I might find peace through the Lord Jesus Christ, for I was as dark upon the point as a stone. My mind wandered off from that to trifles, as the mind will sometimes do when it wishes to keep itself riveted on some all-absorbing topic. Some girls from a charity school, with their white capes and aprons, and their white head-dresses, were passing along, and they drew my attention from the dreadful act of suicide which I was almost premeditating.

"Halloa! what are you doing here?" shouted a man at my elbow.

"It's only me; I am just looking over;" and so I turned and came down. It was then my good fortune to become acquainted with a man who explained what I wished to know. He said,—

"It's all simple enough; God in Christ is reconciling the world unto Himself. Don't you see the simplicity of this? I daresay you are trying to find out all your sins; suppose you did, and put them all down in black and white, what could you do with them better than take them to God, who through Christ has promised to forgive them? Even a Mary Magdalen found mercy, and a Saul of Tarsus found mercy too. You are looking for the thing to be completed when it is already completed. Christ has died the just for the unjust, that He might bring such men as you and I to Himself, and give us a good hope through His resurrection, when we shall rise in the strength of the first resurrection. 'Blessed and holy is he that hath part in the first resurrection.' These are believers in Christ—for the second death shall have no power over them."

This gave me a clearer view of the whole subject; and I present it to my readers, in case any of them may feel now as I felt then. The explanation was so precious that I was frightened I should lose it. All this time I kept the state of my feelings concealed from my wife: I could not get rid of them, and I was ashamed to confess them. At last the truth dawned on my mind, as it dawned on the mind of Luther of old. I was passing along Great Ormond-street one summer's day, forty-seven years ago; a sudden light seemed to illumine the spot where I stood, and near which sat an old apple-woman by her stall. I gave a quick stop, and exclaimed,—

"Glory be to God! now I know that He has pardoned my sins."

The old apple-woman gazed at me with surprise.

"God preserve me!" she exclaimed, "how solemn the man looks!"

I went straight off home, and when I got there I took my wife by the shoulder, and said,—

"Maggie, go down upon your knees and thank God, for I have found salvation."

We knelt down, and I prayed for her, and I prayed for myself.

"Bless my heart, father, I did not know you could pray at all!"

There and then God convinced my wife. I was instrumental in bringing her to the Lord, and when afterwards the ensnarements of drink were likely to lead me away from the Cross, she came in and brought me back to it by showing me an example and signing the Temperance Pledge.

The hour of my conversion I shall never forget, nor the moment when the scales were removed from my eyes, and they beheld the Sun of Righteousness come to my soul with healing in His wings. As I dictate this to my amanuensis, I tell him that this very day before coming to his house, which is very near the spot, I went and stood upon the stone in Ormond-street once more, and anew thanked God for the mercy that had met me there so many years before. The world may laugh at a narrative like this, but the true Christian knows in whom he has believed. The man of science may jeer at a statement of this kind, and call it the ravings of an illiterate enthusiast; but illiterate though I am, and enthusiast though I may be, I have within me that to possess which he would gladly part with his learning and his science. The power I speak of is within me, telling me of a world lost and ruined by the fall; but it also tells me of another and a better one beyond; and it is too vivid, too real, and has lasted too long for it to possess one tinge of romance, or one iota of the poetry which is not founded on the basis of what is true.

MY RELAPSE AND MY SIGNING THE PLEDGE.

Very shortly after my change of heart I sent my children to Great Queen-street Sunday School. Robert went to a school in Westminster. We remained members of the Wesleyan Methodist Society assembling there for some years. Unfortunately my old enemy strong drink overtook me again, whilst employed at the very same work in Theobald's-road where my conversion happened. When the men were paid they used to go to the "White Horse" to get change, and I went along with the rest, but I was not a teetotaler. Just as I was going through the passage the head foreman, who was in the parlour, saw me passing:—

"Come in here, McCurrey," he said; and in the next moment he had handed me the glass of brandy-and-water which was lying before him on the table. I took it to drink his health. He then said,—

"Sit down and have a pipe."

Being called upon to do this by a man in his position I did so, for I thought to myself, "I can't very well say 'no.'" The tempter came in an insidious form, and I fell before his wiles. That night I was taken home drunk to my wife. She was fit to go beside herself with grief. There was I lying drunk in the house, where for a long time past we had been so comfortable. I, who had been one of the visitors of the Strangers' Friend Society, I, who had gone to Guy's Hospital to talk to people about their souls' eternal salvation—there was I lying drunk!

It was a dreadful fall for me. I went to my class-leader about it. He said,—

"Well, Brother McCurrey, what is the matter?"

I told him; but there he was—the man to whom I had gone for advice—sitting with a bottle of gin on the table, and a jug of spring water. He filled up some and handed it to me. He said,—

"You see, Mr. McCurrey, you take too much: take a little now, and it will steady your nerves"—for I was trembling like a leaf.

"It is the accursed little, sir, that is the stumbling-block to me."

"Never mind, you take a little of this, and don't be tempted to take too much."

I took some of what he offered; but need I say that such advice to me was like advice given to a drowning man to save himself without help? I was glad to leave the class-leader's presence; I was glad to leave his church; and I was glad to leave the neighbourhood. I went to reside at Chelsea. I worked here and there, and during this time occurred my experience at St. Katherine's Docks, which I shall elsewhere narrate. It was about this time my very good fortune to meet with a young teetotaler of the name of Harris. Something led me to tell him how I felt, and as we talked together we went over the wooden bridge at Chelsea, to which I shall have often to allude. He said,—

"There are some teetotalers in the Primitive Methodist chapel, and you ought to go and see them."

"Are you one?"

"Yes," he said, "I am."

"Then you won't live long."

"Never mind about me, you look to yourself. I advise you to come with me."

I refused; but when I went home he came after me, and by dint of entreaty he got me to go with him. I heard Mr. Grosjean speaking, and subsequently Mr. Whittaker. The impression these gentlemen produced upon me was very great, and the simplicity of the doctrine they had to propound charmed me. I persuaded my wife to accompany me the next time I went to the Bible Christian chapel, Chelsea.

Oh, as I think of that next time, what a rush of recollections come over me! How large is the lump that rises in my throat, and how husky is the voice that scarcely dares utter the date for the very fulness of joy; and how my heart rises to God in adoration and praise for His wonderful mercies vouchsafed unto me, one of the humblest of men! Let the date I am about to mention be as indelibly written on my tombstone as it is engraved on the tablets of my grateful heart. Dead indeed would it be to all human feeling were I ever to allow that date to be obliterated from my recollection. It was a date on which the fetters of my slavery were struck off, and I stood before the world emancipated and disenthralled. THE 16TH NOVEMBER, 1837. The lecturer, Mr. Grosjean, was eloquent and earnest, and the meeting profoundly impressed. I watched the countenance of my wife as it beamed with the radiance of hope and with the energy of determinate resolve. The lecturer ceased. The voice that had charmed us was heard no more, and then came the time of action. I see her now. I see the noble woman seize the pen, and in unmistakeable characters trace the outlines of her name. The mute appeal was irresistible, and in another moment James McCurrey had signed *the charter of his liberty!* I walked home, and on arriving there I sank upon my knees and prayed to God to help me to keep my vow. It was the first time for a long while since I had prayed before, but the words came from my heart, and the answer found its way into my soul. My wife then prayed that

God would take the love of drink from me. From that day to this I have been an unflinching, uncompromising teetotaler. When I went to bed I could not sleep. Unrefreshed I went to work in the morning; I even had to borrow tools, and then commenced my struggle with the raging appetite within and the strong temptation without. It was a long but a victorious one. The Christmas that ensued was passed in a somewhat cheerless, comfortless manner. I was out of work, for a severe frost had come and stopped all building operation. By some means or other I got enough money to enable my wife to buy some giblets and some pork, and to that six of us sat down on the Christmas-day. After it had been demolished we had a good-sized pudding, and though the plums were a great way apart we managed to dispose of the different ingredients, plums, stones, and all, for we could afford to lose nothing then!

CONSCIENCE.

That Chelsea chapel was long known to me; I believe that some persons who are steeped in sin have gone so far as to say that their consciences never trouble them. If I were to say that it would be a gross untruth. My conscience was always gnawing at me, and at times so great was the effect upon my mind that I was ready to fly from myself; ay! even from life, to escape its upbraidings. Well do I remember on one occasion after a drinking bout, coming home over the wooden bridge at Chelsea; for, I must say here, that where the Victoria Station now stands, used to be a large mass of water, some five or six acres in extent, from which there ran a canal into the Thames. The wooden bridge led into St. George's-road, where I lived. At the present time the bridge has been replaced by a very handsome iron one, which is the admiration of all who see it.

It was a beautiful moonlight night, and the thought came

over me that I was lost, and that for ever and ever; but I cried to God in my anguish and despair, and He saved me. This was about the year 1826, and years before the next turning-point in my life—that of signing the pledge. I knew then that it was the drink that was keeping me back, both socially and spiritually. Whilst all these thoughts were rushing through my mind a policeman came along and broke the spell. He said, "Come, get out of this;" and so I moved on. He must have thought I intended to commit suicide. I went home calmer in my mind than I had been for many a day.

THE FIRE IN THE LOWTHER ARCADE.

Another deliverance I record. Before I signed the pledge there was a great fire in the Lowther Arcade. I was allowed to help the firemen, but being more than three parts stupefied by drink, I walked deliberately into the flames, and fell down a cellar amongst the burning embers. It sobered me in an instant, but how I got out I cannot tell to this day.

CHAPTER III.

A NEW CAREER.—AFTER SIGNING THE PLEDGE.—TRIALS, TEMPTATIONS, AND PERSECUTIONS.

THAT little Bible Christian chapel over the wooden bridge, Chelsea, has a place in my very warmest remembrances. There I signed. There the first Female Total Abstinence Society, in the western suburb of London, Chelsea, Pimlico, and Brompton, was formed. My friend, Mr. James Balfour, a month before had signed at Hemming's-row, having been known as a convivial ringleader in the district, and afterwards as an energetic worker and firm advocate of the cause of sobriety. His wife, Mrs. Balfour, signed in that little chapel (October 16), and her name was the ninth on the list that autumn. Before that winter was over the society numbered 1500. My wife, Mrs. Barron, Mrs. Tracey, Mrs. Alsop, and Mrs. Balfour were on the committee of ladies, and began a system of home visitation of those who signed the pledge, which I believe, under God, was one great means of keeping the society together and promoting its success. But to return to my own individual experiences.

It was not very easy then, compared with the present time, to profess and practise total abstinence. Jeers and insults of all kinds had to be endured, not only from drunkards—nay, seldom to any great extent from them, for if they opposed, the reason of their doing so was so obvious that it was soon seen by all; besides, these poor drunkards in their ill health, poverty, recklessness, and general misery furnished the most powerful argument for teetotalism. But it was the moderate, respectable, self-satisfied, and religious people whose opposition was hard to bear. Even yet, though the tone of society is altered, they are my most obstinate adversaries; and whether they mean it or not, they are too often the antagonists of truth and the champions of error.

A working man who then (1837) became an abstainer had to face also the keenest opposition from his shopmates. He was watched and taunted, often his clothes and tools injured. I had my full share of this to bear.

PLEDGING MY CLOTHES.

One day, when at work at Cubitt's, and very shortly after I became a teetotaler, I missed my coat. This was only one of the petty annoyances to which I was subjected by men who saw that I was getting on, and who had not the courage to give up their connexion with the drink. I did not quite break off all the old associations, for though I used to drink no beer, I used to "stand a pot" when my turn came. One day, however, this was put a stop to by an Irishman on the works, who said,—

"You're a fine teetotaler, paying your pot o' beer!"

I said, "You will never have to say that any more."

The nasty feeling which had existed amongst the men from the very moment I signed the pledge was increased by my refusal to pay for any more beer. This particular winter happened to be a very hard one, and the Marquis of Westminster gave some money to Mr. Cubitt for distribution among his men. The sums were distributed to men in the first, second, and third classes; and although I was only in the third class, Mr. Thomas Cubitt put me down in the first class, so that I got something like 3*l*. 5*s*. I bought a new coat amongst other things with my money. This was the coat which, unknown to me, had been taken by some of the men and pledged for drink. I never rested till I made the men who pledged it restore it. The deputy foreman was one of the chief movers in this exploit, but, poor fellow! a little later on in his career, he was discharged for drunkenness, and the drink ultimately killed him.

The opposition of my felloww-orkmen was also shown in putting me to the hardest work and in the most dangerous places. I hope I have a deep and true sense of the rights of labour and the interests of working men, but I am bound to confess that my experience in my early days of teetotalism, convinced me that no tyranny practised towards them by the wealthy and powerful, is so great as that which they often practise on their fellow-workmen, and even on themselves. Drink is their real tyrant. One of my earliest jobs of work, which many watched me at, hoping I might fall, was a difficult test to a new convert. Instead of a defeat it became a triumph.

THE OVEN.

Soon after I signed the pledge, I was employed as a journeyman at Mr. Cubitt's, and encountered a great deal of opposition. The head foreman was hard upon me, though, poor man, he has since died from the effects of drink. About two years after I became a teetotaler, the jealousy of me got so high that a plan was formed to give me what they called "a roasting." Of this plan the foreman was perfectly aware. A letter came from the head office—or was said to have come from there—which the foreman read to me. He said,—

"You know Mr. ———, the baker at Thames Bank?"

"Yes."

"Go down there to-night to draw the tiles, repair the furnace, and put it into working order, and Charles Refroy will go with you."

Charles Refroy was an enemy of mine, but not such an inveterate one as some of them were. He used often to say, "There is no mistake but what you are on the right side." I was therefore very glad that it was he who was with me. We went to the place, got into the baker's shop, and down the stairs we went. I found that the small bread had just been taken out of the oven; it was half-past five in the afternoon. I went into the oven, and the heat was tremendous. I tumbled in my tiles in a minute, and then rushed out. The mortal fear I had was that they would lock me in. I however came out, lay down, and had a rest. The baker's wife came down and offered me some drink, but I said I would prefer tea. She accordingly came down with a very nice bason of tea and two rounds of bread-and-butter, and I felt "a man and a half better."

Charles Refroy had his turn in the oven, and soon came out more dead than alive. I went in again in the tremendous heat, and came out once more, and had a fresh supply of tea. Charles Refroy, who had had spirits, was at last obliged to declare that he could go in no more, and I was forced to stay and finish the job. When it was all done, I had a thorough good wash, and I believe the tremendous perspiration into which it threw me, cleansed me from the impurities of the drink which still lingered in my system. The baker paid us, and off we went, the work having taken us from the time already mentioned until eight o'clock on the Sunday morning.

When I got home I found my wife in a terrible state, not knowing the reason of my absence. She feared that I had broken my pledge, and she went round a number of the public-houses to see if she could get any trace of me. One man, whom I afterwards made a teetotaler, was asked by my wife it he had seen me anywhere, and he had the cruelty to reply,—

"Yes; he is fighting along with a soldier at the 'Old Nell Gwynn.'"

I opened our door and said, "How are you getting on here?"

She flew into my arms, and crying bitterly, said, "What did you go and take the drink for?"

I had more trouble to persuade my wife that I was sober and not drunk than I can well describe. It was a black job with her.

"Mother!" I said, "I have not been drinking."

I gave her the money, and that looked a little more convincing than anything else. I had a long sleep; and when I woke up, instead of feeling the worse for my work, I felt quite refreshed.

The winter that followed my signing the pledge, I have said, was one of great severity. There were four feet of snow on the ground, and altogether I felt it much, as I was very poor. I was also discharged from my employment, and was in much distress.

One day I was met by Mr. Harris, the man who had persuaded me to sign the pledge, and was asked by him how I was getting on. I told him; and he at once said, "If a sovereign is of any use to you, you are welcome to the loan of one; but I can't afford to give it to you." I refused, feeling very much abashed, and went home and told my wife, who said I ought to have taken it. A few days after I met Harris again, and this time I borrowed the sovereign from him. Here then was all my capital, and what was I to do with it? I spoke to the manager of the Equitable Gas Works about going through the streets selling coke, but I told him I had no sacks. He said he would lend them to me. My boy went round with me, and I managed to live very fairly in this way until the spring of the following year. I drew the first three sacks over the very piece of ground where my house in Dorset-street, Pimlico, now stands.

Soon after I signed the pledge, I was employed by Mr. Cubitt to help in making the tide-wall of the Thames. Here, of course, beer was handed round as usual. My share was placed beside me, and everything done to provoke me to drink it. At last, being greatly annoyed, I struck the can a rather heavy blow, which not only upset the beer but destroyed the can which held it. I was called "over the coals" for this; but, on representing the state of affairs, I was allowed a bottle of gingerbeer and a slice of bread-and-cheese instead.

FALLING OFF A LADDER.

I fell off a ladder in Pimlico. At the time this happened I was doing some lime-whiting when I was in a little way of business for myself. The pail of whiting was above me, and the ladder was shaking. The pail was shaken off the click, and I fell, and the contents of the pail fell over me. The distance I fell was nearly six or seven feet. I was blind for some time, and was attended to spiritually by the Rev. Dr. Tracey. He and I fell out before this, and I will explain how this came about. He was a Dissenting minister in Chelsea, and a stanch teetotaler as well. He, together with Dr. Burns and Mr. J. W. Green, held a very large meeting in Theobald's-road. At the meeting Dr. Tracey was present, and it seems that somebody told him I was an infidel. When he was called upon to preside he said, "I cannot address this meeting or preside over it if this Mr. McCurrey is going to speak, for he is an infidel."

Dr. Burns rose up and said, "I beg your pardon, we know James McCurrey, and we know further that you are wrongly informed."

In the meantime Dr. Tracey had gone so far as to move out of the chair, and Dr. Burns had enough to do to keep me in my seat. Dr. Tracey was persuaded by those present that I was not an infidel, and when my turn came Dr. Burns called upon me to speak. The Doctor did so in these words,—

"We call upon our metropolitan builder to speak."

I did speak, and said what I ought not to have said.

"Mr. Chairman, with all due respect to you, you have wounded me very much. You have publicly said that I was an infidel, when you ought to have ascertained the fact—if it was a fact—from my own lips in private. I am not an infidel, but I am a thorough teetotaler. Whatever people may say about me, this is what I can truly say about you, that you have been a great sinner, and but for the mercy of God you would have been in hell. All I wished of you was that you would give me the same chance that Almighty God gave you, to answer for myself and to repent; but you knocked me down, and would have turned me out, because somebody else told you a falsehood."

He settled the matter by saying, "I admit I am wrongly informed."

I then went on with my speech, and said nothing more about the matter. This brought me again into connexion with Dr. Tracey when I fell off the ladder, and when I was not so well off pecuniarily as I subsequently was. He called to see me when I was ill, but I could not see him because the lime had blinded me.

He said, "Do you know who I am?"

I said, "Yes, sir, you are Dr. Tracey; you know that we have eyes of the flesh and spiritual eyes."

He said, "Don't be excited."

In consequence of the numerous questions he asked, I told him a tale about my eldest daughter. I said,—

"I have got a large family. I bought one of my girls a nice box of clothes when I became steady, and got her, as I thought, into a very good situation in a gentleman's house in Albemarle-street. He used to attend St. James's Church. She was obliged to go every Sunday morning to carry the Bibles and sit behind him. She came home and told her mother and myself that she didn't like the place. She told us that the very people she was sitting behind at church in the Sunday morning played at cards on the Sunday night. I went to the house to ascertain the truth of this story. I knocked at the door, and one of the servants opened it. I said to her, 'You have a young servant here named Jane McCurrey, who came here three or four months ago?' She said they had. 'Well,' said I, 'I want to ask you a question. Do the same people who go to church in the morning from this house play at cards in the evening?' 'Oh!' said the servant, 'that is nothing here!' 'Then, Jane,' I said, 'where is your box?' 'It is upstairs.' 'Show me the way.' 'You must not take her away without giving notice.' 'Notice! they shall have no notice from me.' I shouldered her trunk and brought it home with her; and here she is, box and all. I never heard anything more about it from the parties with whom she was."

The Doctor said, "And is this your girl?"

I said, "Yes, sir, it is."

"Well," he said, "we want a servant."

"If she will suit, you are very welcome to her."

She stayed there until she was married some nine years after. Dr. Tracey became her banker, and when she left she had saved a sum getting on towards 70*l*. But religious persecution was worst of all; it led to

MY EXPULSION FROM THE CHAPEL.

At the time this event happened I was no doubt a decided

nuisance to a great many persons who, though well meaning in their way, cared very little for teetotalism, and much less for me on account of it. At last my co-worshippers decided that I must either give up my membership or cease causing a "turmoil," as they termed it, on the Sabbath-day. I went to see the late Rev. James Sherman about it.

"Mr. McCurrey," he said, "wherever you feel yourself most happy, that is the place for you to be, and I believe that you are as much called to this work as I am to the ministry—only I could not do your work, and you could not do mine. You are right in doing it, and I advise you to remain in it."

I was consequently expelled from the church for speaking in the open air on Temperance.

Eighteen months after that I was going home one Sunday night, and it began to rain. I said to the friends who were with me, "Let's go into this chapel." It was the old one I used to attend, but in the interval (having been expelled from it) I attended another. I went in; my four friends followed me. The minister said,—

"I have very much pleasure in seeing our friend and brother Mr. McCurrey here to-night, and I am sure he will be glad to hear what I am going to tell him. I myself have been now going on fifteen months a total abstainer, and I hope he will come back amongst us."

He gave out the hymn, and then called upon me to pray. I shook like a leaf as I obeyed his mandate. I thanked God that He had convinced the minister that it was his duty to sign the pledge for the sake of the perishing ones around him, and I prayed further that his people might also see it to be their duty to follow his example.

At the close of the service the minister and several of the people came forward and shook me warmly by the hand, and more than one said, "God bless you, Mr. McCurrey!"

CHAPTER IV.

RECORDS OF MY CHILDREN.

At the time I signed the pledge my family consisted of my wife and four surviving children, out of a family of six. They were James, Jane, Robert, and Margaret. Of these dear ones—all now gone—three were all that I could wish. Jane resembled her mother in earnestness of character. She had seen the sorrow that drink had wrought in our home, and was quite old enough to form her own opinions on the evil, and to rejoice in the change. My own experience is that the young, unless greatly perverted, always readily and zealously adopt our principles. My dear girl was a very great comfort to her mother. She was a sincere Christian from her youth up, and married early in life a consistent teetotaler, Mr. Cable; and after living happily with him many years, being the mother of several lovely children, it pleased God to remove her in the prime of her days (aged forty-six—1870) from her mourning family, and me, her sorrowing father. Truly, "God moves in a mysterious way."

My son James was taken by his uncle, Mr. Clark, and was brought up to be a dentist. He was a fine-looking, clever youth, and, in the midst of my unhappy drinking career, it was yet managed, doubtless by my dear wife, that he should have some advantages of education. His talent and address made his uncle take to him; and it was naturally thought a great matter when we were so sunk in poverty, and to all appearance utterly ruined in worldly prospects, that our eldest son should be learning a gentlemanly profession, with every prospect of success in it.

I shall have to give the history of my brother-in-law as part of my life's experiences: when that is read it will not be wonderful that my poor boy, James, was early led to know the taste of strong drink, so as to hanker for it, even when he for a time adopted total abstinence. I fear sobriety was never with him a principle. He had good impulses—I confess I have lived to distrust mere impulse; nothing but a firm resolve to be thorough-going and stanch, holding the truth with a grip, as in God's sight, and for life or death, is really to be relied on amid the temptations—the thousandfold temptations—strong drink presents.

The demon of intemperance, that I was fighting against with all my might, ensnared my eldest son. His brief life, which began so prosperously, was saddened and shortened by drink, and his name and memory is to me an abiding sorrow.

I shall have incidentally to mention my poor son at a later period, when I record the fate of several members of my wife's family, with whom his lot unfortunately was cast. I have the deepest reason to denounce strong drink, for, though by the blessing of God, and the help of a good wife, I was able to struggle out of the clutches of the demon of intemperance, many whom I loved and would have done anything to rescue were victims. And it has ever been, and is, a serious drawback to my comfort, that I have had in m family connexions to pay a heavy tribute in heart, hope, and means, to the destroyer.

My son Robert, a brave, strong, sturdy boy of eight when I signed, was for some time seriously thinking about the great change in our home. The dear lad was pleased, for joy had come to the fireside, warmth to the hearth, plenty to the cupboard, and, more than all, peace and hope to his anxious mother's heart. He understood the blessed change, and no doubt contrasted it in his youthful mind with the sorrow and want that his childhood had been but too familiar with. But he for a time expressed no great desire to sign the pledge. There were no Bands of Hope then; but it must not be supposed we neglected the children. There were some juvenile gatherings in 1838, one in particular at Cook's Ground Chapel, Chelsea, where Mr. Balfour's little daughter (now Mrs. Dawson Burns) was just able to write enough to sign her name.

But as very early in my out-of-door advocacy I was called to encounter opposition, when one day I was taken off by the police for speaking to the people at the "White Stiles," my son Robert followed me to the station-house, and in all the enthusiasm of youthful resolution signed the pledge, and kept it from that time forth until his lamented death at the age of forty-one. He was ever a most consistent, industrious young man; and as by God's blessing I made my way up the steep hill Difficulty, until I scaled one of the headlands of Success, I was able to help Robert. He was of my own trade, and my right hand for many a year, until he became a master-man for himself.

As I am dealing now with private matters before entering on my public career, I may briefly say of my dear son that he was "diligent in business, fervent in spirit, serving the Lord." He prospered greatly; but in the year '48 he met with an accident, a fall in a building. We did not think much of it at the time, but his spine was hurt; and, though he had the best skill that could be got, he declined. He suffered very much but very patiently, and, in 1870, died at forty-one, full of peace in believing. He left a wife, but no family. He showed his love for the temperance cause by leaving 600*l.* to it, and several other legacies to hospitals; provided for his wife, and left the bulk of his property to his sister Jane's children—as thus recorded:—

MR. ROBERT McCURREY.

"Died, July 20th, after a long and painful illness, from an attack of paralysis, brought on by a fall some years since, at the early age of forty-one, deeply regretted by his friends, Mr. Robert McCurrey, the son of the well-known temperance advocate, Mr. James McCurrey. He had been an abstainer thirty-two years. After providing for his family, he did not forget the benevolent institutions of his country; he has left 100*l.* each to St. George's, Westminster, and Consumptive Hospitals, 100*l.* to the Strangers' Friend Society, and 600*l.* to the Total Abstinence cause."—*Temperance Record*.

Our youngest, my sweet Maggie, was the angel in our house for many a year. None that looked upon her beautiful, blooming face could think that a blight was to come on our cherished flower, the fairest in our home-garden: therefore the Master chose her just when she was loveliest.

"I was dumb, I opened not my mouth, because Thou didst it."

I cannot pursue the theme of my private sorrows, but I subjoin an account of my

LITTLE MARGARET.

My little Margaret was eleven years old when she died. She was a teetotaler, and, indeed, I do not think she ever touched drink. She used always to be talking about her teetotal father, and I was very fond of her. When I was out she could generally reckon on something being brought her by me when I came back. She used to sit within the door-way watching for me, and welcome me by singing little hymns. I sent her to a boarding-school at Lewes, where she remained for a couple of years, and was getting on very well; but, alas! that fell disease consumption was slowly, but surely, undermining her constitution. When she came home on the last Christmas of her life, she did not seem to enjoy herself at all as she usually did. She used to lay about the fire, and lounge on the sofa. That went on until she went to bed, and then she became like a skeleton. She had a voice like an angel, and it was truly delightful to hear her sing. The doctor, of course, was in attendance upon her. He encouraged us for a time by saying that she might get better; but, at last, he was obliged to say that there was absolutely no hope.

"The other lung is affected, and you must do as well as you can for her until she passes away."

Her mother said,—

"Doctor, is there anything you could give her that would relieve her at all?"

"Well," he said, "yes; give her a tablespoonful of wine with the white of an egg in it."

God only knows how I felt; but my little girl decided the matter without a word being spoken,—

"No, no; I don't want any wine. I know the wine can't save me, and I know I am going to be with Jesus, which is far better, and I will not take it. Teetotalism has given me a good father and a good mother, and I won't touch it."

Neither would she on any account. Her words before her death were rather those of the experience of age than the carelessness of childhood. She called us all round the bed, and said,—

Margaret's Happy End.

"Sit down, and let me compose myself. I just want one thing: will you go and tell Dr. Love (the doctor who attended her) I want to see him?"

Some one went, and he came immediately. She said,—

"I wanted to see you, Dr. Love. Did you think I was angry with you when I spoke so sharply about the wine?"

"Oh no, Margaret; I know you suffer a good deal."

"I want to ask you to forgive me if I hurt your feelings."

He said,—

"Oh no, you didn't hurt my feelings at all."

She then turned round and said,—

"If you don't look at me, I will sing you a hymn."

She sang right through the hymn, commencing—

> "In that beautiful place,
> He has gone to prepare."

When I think of the scene it moves me to my very centre, even at this distance of time. It was about a day before she died that this interview took place. At the last she shook me by the hand, and said,—

"I know I am going to Jesus, my Saviour and Redeemer."

At the last gasp she waved her hand as though in victory.

"Thanks be to God, which giveth us the victory through our Lord Jesus Christ."

CHAPTER V.

OPEN-AIR ADVOCACY.—ITS COMMENCEMENT IN CHELSEA.—PUBLIC-HOUSE CORNERS.—"WHITE STILES."—ITINERATING IN WESTMINSTER, SEVEN DIALS.—DRUNKEN PEOPLE.—SUMMARY OF WORK.

I MAY say here, that from the time of my conversion I had a very great reverence for the Sabbath-day; something, too, of the outer reverence I had seen paid to the Sabbath in my youth in Scotland had impressed me, although there was that private drinking in my parents' dwelling, which does so much in Scotland still to neutralize the influence of Sabbath observances and religious teaching.

I knew it was lawful to do good on the Sabbath-day. That was clear to me; and also that if a working-man was to have time to devote to his fellow-man, it must be by taking the hallowed hours of the Sabbath, both to do good and get good. Hence, early in the year that followed my signing the pledge (1838), in the hours before, between, or after Divine service, I took the opportunity of speaking to those who would listen, on the evils of drinking the drunkard's drink.

The public-houses were not then closed in the morning hours of the Sabbath. Terrible scenes used to be witnessed at the doors of public-houses as well as inside. Idle, drunken men lounging about; poor, trembling women waiting for their husbands to come out, or imploring for some trifle of money to be saved from the clutches of the publican. It would scarcely be believed now, the disorder and misery that were seen then.

I was very strong in health, and I had also a strong voice; both were needful. Some of my temperance friends saw with me, that if we were to pluck brands from the burning we must not be afraid to go near the fire. So I and Mr. James Balfour, who also had signed the pledge in the previous autumn, began the work in Chelsea of outdoor advocacy.

We first tried distributing tracts at the public-house doors; but many could not read, others lit their pipes with them. Speaking to them was the right and the only course. Accordingly, I began at a corner opposite a public-house. Of course I was opposed; but the poor drunkards were startled, and they listened at first in a stupefied wonder, then intelligently. When I got hoarse—for open-air speaking is very exhausting—then my friend Balfour (a Zaccheus in stature, but with a stentorian voice) would take up the theme. The publican would send out his men and hirelings to interrupt, and often took advantage of Mr. Balfour's stature to throw something over him or crowd round him so as to drown his voice. But one Sunday morning I well recollect when my friend, with all his pluck, was nearly overcome. A respectable woman living near the publican brought out a strong wooden chair, planted it in her little front garden, and, calling to Mr. Balfour, placed it at his service. Raised on this, and no doubt pleased with the kindness of the lady, my zealous friend made himself so well heard, and caused such a deep impression for good, that from that time until 1841, when he went on a mission to the Channel Islands, he was one of the most effective open-air speakers, and a great help in the work I had so greatly at heart, the establishing of regular open-air meetings. One of our very valued adherents was Mr. Harper. He signed in 1840, and helped our cause in the very hard work of that time. Our plan soon was to divide in the morning, from nine to eleven, the hour of Divine service, and, going different ways, to catch hold of the drunkards gathering about the public-houses, speak to them, and get them to go to the "White Stiles," King's-road, in the afternoon. In this way we itinerated into Sloane-square, Jew's-row, and the lower parts of Chelsea, with the good result that many were induced to come in the afternoon.

THE "WHITE STILES" MEETINGS.

In the course of this narrative frequent mention has been made of the meetings which we used to hold at the "White Stiles," and also of sundry incidents which occurred there, and which, as a record of progress, are thought worthy of a place in this production. It would be most ungrateful if I did not acknowledge with the most heartfelt gratitude the assistance I received from such men as Jabez Inwards, Richard Nash Bailey, the Rev. S. Beardsall, and also a great many others, whose names are mentioned elsewhere in the course of this narrative. The "White Stiles" was a sort of rendezvous for the old teetotalers. They used to come there to address the meetings on the Sunday, and would then go home with me to tea. People on all sides acknowledged the good which these meetings were doing, and the living evidence of it was to be seen nearly every time we assembled. Notwithstanding this a petition was sent round for signatures to induce the authorities of Chelsea College to stop the meetings, for the ground I spoke on was included in their property. As usual, we held a meeting there one Sunday afternoon, when there was a tremendous row, caused by the arrival on the scene of a couple of policemen. Of course I refused to go with them, and after some bother they

THE "WHITE-STILES" MEETING.

retired. The next day I had a letter from Sir John Wilson, who was then at the head of the College, to say that he wished to see me. I was rather frightened at this, but I waited upon him at the appointed time and place.

"I wished to see you, Mr. McCurrey," he began, "because I have received some letters about you couched in very strong language. I should like, therefore, to know about this matter. I have been to some of your meetings and listened to you, and am very sorry that the people are determined to have you removed. The committee of the hospital think well of you, and I may go so far as to say that I have spoken in your favour. If they do remove you, I will find you a place somewhere else; but in the meantime we will try and see what is to be done where we are. Don't you think, if you were to preach the Gospel, it would be much better?"

"No, sir, I do not. Poor wandering drunkards would not be able to appreciate its glorious truths. They want clothes upon their backs, and food in their stomachs, before they will be in a fit state to hear and believe."

"I know," he said, "they are a most disreputable lot, and so are most of my pensioners, I am sorry to say."

"You are right, sir; but we have made fourteen of them teetotalers, including Captain Newdon, whom perhaps you know."

I also mentioned the names of one or two more. Sir John appeared very much astonished.

"I am downright glad to hear it!" he cried very heartily. "Your name is a Scotch one. What countryman are you?"

"I am a Scotchman."

"Have you ever been in the army?"

"No, sir, only in the militia."

"Well, I may tell you now that I have brought your case before the board. I told them that for the last five years you had opened your meetings punctually as the clock struck three. Is that so?"

"It is, sir."

"Well, that punctuality was a very great commendation of you in their eyes. But, let me ask, do you come from Glasgow?"

"I do, sir; and speaking of the army, I may say that most of my friends are in the army. I had two uncles in the Peninsular war; one fell at Salamanca, and the other at Toulouse."

"McCurrey, McCurrey!" he said, thinking, and tapping his forehead.

I assisted his memory by saying, "One of my uncles was an ensign and the other was a private."

"Did he belong to such a regiment—the one that fell at Toulouse?"

"He did."

"Then I was within a few yards of him when he fell, and if you are only as good a man as your uncle was, you will be a credit to your country."

It was astonishing to see the warmth with which he spoke to me after that. I had no idea that my departed uncles were ever destined to do me so much service. I then told him of the annoyance to which I had been subjected by persons who were selling all kinds of fruit, and that it was they who created the disturbances, and not myself. He told me to go on holding my meetings until he communicated with me further.

The next Sunday I opened the meeting as usual by giving out a hymn. The "man in blue" came up as before, and told me to "move on."

I said, "If you don't mind what you are up to, you will drop in for it. I am authorized to stand here by Sir John Wilson, and if you don't mind I'll lock *you* up as sure as you are a living man."

Up started one of the pensioners and said, "That's quite true. You'd better mind what you're about. He's got the power to stand here, and no one can remove him."

And so it turned out. I stood there for nearly three years after that. In Chelsea College we had thirty or forty teetotalers, and Sir John himself came out in his carriage and pair, with his wife and daughters, to listen to me, thus showing to those whom it might concern that I was a recognized "Institution" of the College.

A man met me on one occasion who said, "You inoculated me into teetotalism at the 'White Stiles,' Chelsea, at a time when I hadn't a sixpence. I signed the pledge at one of your open-air meetings there fifteen years ago, and am doing well, as you may judge from the fact that I have now three houses."

MY WORK AT THE GREEN PARK, FACING THE DUKE OF YORK'S MONUMENT.

Coming home one day from a meeting at the Seven Dials, I saw a great crowd following the drums and fifes of a military band. I looked for a time, and in spite of their gay regimentals I pitied the poor soldiers from the bottom of my heart. I said to myself,—

"If these men only knew what I know, would they be in that position?"

It was evident they were marching from one barracks to another. A Primitive Methodist lady, with a few others who were with me, said,—

"Mr. McCurrey, how can these people know unless God sends some one to teach them?"

I said,—

"I wish He would send somebody."

"I believe," said the lady, "He has sent you this morning. Get up and speak to them: God will help you."

Without another word, up I got, and, taking out my hymn-book, began,—

"Rise and shine," &c.

I sang it as the soldiers passed, and some of those who were not under marching orders stayed behind. I should think that altogether I collected an audience of about 150 people. I kept them for about an hour; but in the midst of my talking two or three of the members of the Society of Friends came up, who had been attending their meeting in St. Martin's-lane. I happened to say,—

"I have been a teetotaler three years, and I want every one of you to sign the pledge."

They seemed very favourably impressed.

At that first meeting I got seven or nine signatures, and the meetings went on for three years and a half. I gave this work up because some one came to help me, and being freed here I was able to go and commence work elsewhere.

I did so, the result being that many young recruits signed the pledge.

AT THE "GOAT AND BOOTS."

At one time of my career I used to be very much annoyed by the pot-boy of the "Goat and Boots," who, on one occasion, declared that I had been drinking gin-and-water. I promised him that he should hear more about it. He didn't know what I meant, but I very soon let him. I invited some of my followers to accompany me to a certain rendezvous opposite the "Goat and Boots." I had a most useful temperance man with me at the time, named James Reynell, or, as he was called, Jemmy the Greek, whose services to the temperance cause ought never to be forgotten: I can never mention the names of old veterans like Reynell, Richard Noah Bailey,

Esterbrooke, and Hatfield, without a feeling of thankfulness to God that I was privileged to have the countenance and support of such true-hearted men. Reynell, who was particularly identified with me in this exploit, was only a labourer when he became a teetotaler, and always attributed his conversion to me. Any one who touched me he used to threaten with "a clout on the ear," and as he was a strong-built fellow, with a rather uncomfortable look of determination about the eye, very few dared so much as to try and molest me when he was present. On arriving within twenty or thirty yards of the "Goat and Boots" we made the arrangements for the meeting. I admit it was not a wise thing to do, but it was done, and there's an end of it. I borrowed a chair from an old Irishman. He said,—

"Are you going to speak on teetotalism?"

"I am," I replied.

"God bless you!" he said, "then I will give you a chair."

Immediately the meeting began, the disturbance which lasted all through the proceedings began too. Out came the publican and the pot-boy, and the noise thus made ended in my being taken to the station-house by the police, with some thirty of the people as a body-guard. Mr. Lowrie, the superintendent, was at the station-house when I arrived. Evidence was given by several respectable witnesses as to the disgraceful language which the publican and his pot-boy had used towards me, as a man who was simply trying to do all the good he could amongst his own class. Amongst other things evidence was borne to the fact, that he swore that if he had a knife he would cut my throat. The superintendent said he could not have all this disturbance, but nothing was done to me, and I was not locked up as they had threatened. The people were all waiting to hear the result. Those who had watches, or, as they were called, "teetotal blossoms," were ready to pawn them to bail me out. There was such a turn-out on this occasion as I hardly ever created before. Numbers of those who had been benefited by the temperance cause were of course vehement in my favour; but numbers more, and amongst them many religious people, said I ought to be stopped. When I came out I got to the corner of the bridge, where I saw a woman lying upon the towing-path dead. The blood was coming out of her mouth and ears. Although I had just been cautioned by the superintendent, and although the terrors of the law were hanging over me, my very spirit was stirred within me at this horrible sight. Something of the spirit which animated the Apostle Paul on Mars Hill was kindled in my soul. Looking down upon and pointing to her, I then turned to the people who were around, and said,—

"Here is some of drink's handiwork. Here lies this woman who, in all probability, would be the happy mother of a happy family, and the watchful guardian of a happy fireside, but for the demon drink."

I then went on to warn the people of their danger, and urged them to give up tampering with strong drink. The tears ran down my cheeks in streams, and I was afterwards assured that the address which was there delivered had an effect upon some of the people present which nothing seemed to have had before. The scene before me, and the incidents which were known to surround me, refuted in the most complete manner some of the calumnies which had been uttered before the police superintendent, and on the space before the "Goat and Boots."

MY WORK AT SEVEN DIALS.

Seven Dials does not enjoy the best of reputations in the present day; but at the time when I used to visit it, it would require the pencil of another Hogarth to depict the deplorable condition in which it was. I was always in the habit of speaking in the open air, and many a time was I threatened for so doing by the minions of the law. I used to attend the religious meetings of some good Primitive Methodist women at Chelsea, and to them I announced my intention of opening another meeting, and I said, "I want you to come and sing for me." They agreed, and on the appointed Sunday morning we started for the scene of action. When I got there I could not get anything to stand upon. This was in 1839, and all the public-houses and shops were open all day at that time. I went into a bacon shop and borrowed an egg-box, and left the man threepence for the loan of it. It was under these circumstances that I commenced a work which lasted three years. The meetings were largely and regularly attended, and I believe are continued more or less now. I am sure that one half of those who now conduct them do not know that I commenced them more than thirty years ago.

To resume, however. I mounted this egg-box. We got on very nicely. There were no signatures, but in this respect I got on better afterwards. The police, as usual, wanted to remove me, but I said, "I won't be removed; I am doing no harm here." I ultimately gained my point, but there was certainly a tremendous row; yet a large number of persons signed the pledge. I went on talking away on the top of this egg-box, and very soon the meeting consisted of at least 2000 persons. I very often used to pull my watch out and call it a "teetotal blossom." I did so on this occasion. One fellow said, "I know the time when you wouldn't keep that long."

"There," I cried, "is my witness!"

In the midst of all this I observed a cab driving full tilt at the meeting. Four people were inside and four or five were outside smoking long pipes. They were Irishmen. They came up hurrahing as loud as they could, and declaring that they would ride down the Methodist preacher. Their oaths and curses were fearful. Several of the people, however, caught hold of the horse's head, turned it, and sent the cab off in another direction. After that we finished our meeting in about half an hour. We sang that morning, "Praise God from whom all blessings flow." I started it, and, quite to my surprise, the people joined in.

One Christmas-day, after these meetings had been held for some time, or rather the day before Christmas, Thomas Whittaker was going to preach a sermon in St. Clement's-lane schoolroom in the afternoon, and he took for his text, "Behold, I stand at the door and knock." A great number went to hear him preach this sermon, and amongst them was a man named Trower, whom I had never seen to my knowledge before. When I came out of the building, after hearing Mr. Whittaker preach, this man came up to me and said,—

"Well, Mr. Currey, how do you do?"

I should say that it was very often the custom to drop the first part of my name in the way this man did it.

"Thank you," I said, "I am pretty well."

"My good lady told me to come here and ask you to have a cup of tea with us."

After a few more words I went with him and his grandchildren, for he had two of them in his hand. He took me into Monmouth-street, Seven Dials; and when I got so far, I began to doubt, and said, "Where are you going to?" I was really afraid he was going to lead me into a trap. When we got about halfway on, one of the girls said, pointing up, "That's our window, lighted up with candles."

He knocked at the door, and as soon as it was opened the little girl rushed up, crying out, "He's coming, grandmother! he's coming, grandmother!"

I got upstairs, and was invited to enter the room, which I did. The wife had her hand tied in a sling.

She said, "I am very glad to see you. Has Thomas told you? Well, if he hasn't, what he could not say I can. What a stupid fellow, not to tell you that he became a teetotaler, the morning that the cab was going to drive you down with the men in it!"

Here, then, was the secret of this grateful man's pressing invitation. It was a comfortable party. We sat round a long table, or rather two tables put together, and there was his son, and his son's wife and two children, and there was the daughter and her husband, and two or three more children. In fact, we were no less than nine or ten in number. It was while the meal was proceeding that the poor woman thus expressed herself:—

"That morning that you were going to be driven down by those boot-closers, my poor husband had been drinking for about seven weeks, and was ashamed to come home; but you told him there were more men separated from their wives through drink than through anything else in the universe, and you invited him to turn back, and if he had done wrong try to do better. In this, you said, God would help him, for He had said, 'Though your sins be as scarlet, they shall be as white as snow; though they be red like crimson, they shall be as wool.' He had been a pious man previously, and you assured him that though his inward lusts rebelled, yet the weepings of victorious grace would lead Christ to slay his sins."

This idea was borrowed from the hymn,—

> "The inward lusts rebel;
> Oh! 'tis but a struggle, gasp of life,
> The weepings of victorious grace
> Shall slay thy sins and end the strife."

"Come on, my lad," I said, "and sign the pledge."

He went to Ship-yard and signed the pledge, and told them that he had listened to a bricklayer who persuaded him to become a member. At the time I took tea with him he had been a member for about four or five months, and ultimately became exceedingly useful. He used to take charge of a hall there—Denmark-street Hall—where I had spoken. His wife is dead and gone to glory, and all his sons, I believe, are doing well. I was speaking about his case in the large hall in Westminster, but didn't know he was there. I was therefore surprised when he afterwards stood up and said, "Mr. McCurrey does not know I am present, but I stand up to thank God that I can bear my testimony to every word he has said, and I am now a teetotaler going on for seven years."

I employed him subsequently, and we have been friends ever since.

At the same meeting, in Seven Dials, there was present a man from Wellingborough, who had absented himself from his wife for nearly six weeks, during which time she did not know where he was. He returned home to that town, leaving me in ignorance not only of his history, but of the very fact that he had attended the meeting.

Mr. Jabez Inwards was in Wellingborough speaking with his usual power, and after he had gone they sent for me. They were mostly shoemakers who lived there, and, being a very rough-and-ready lot, and a little difficult to manage, the friends wanted me to come down and see if I could do anything with them. Mr. Burn, a silversmith, and a member of the Society of Friends, would not let me hold open-air meetings. However, to return. I went down by coach, starting from the "Bells," then a somewhat famous posting-house. It was a winter morning, and such a one as I shall probably remember to the last day of my life. The message I received from Wellingborough was as follows:—"You must go outside, as the people cannot afford to pay inside fare." It was with anything but comfortable feelings that I mounted the seat, and by the time I got off to get my dinner I was benumbed. It was half-past nine o'clock at night that I arrived in Wellingborough, instead of being half-past six. The snow was so heavy about me that when I got off I could not stir. I stood like a fool, not knowing where to go or what to do. I knew nobody, and had nothing but my working clothes on. A stranger took me to a place where I was likely to get a bed— a coffee-shop; and I remember now there were three compartments or stalls in the eating department.

I said, " I will have a cup of coffee."

A woman with a very strange look about her brought me a penny bun with some currants in it.

Some one said, " She is a little queer, but quite harmless."

" Have you seen Williams?" she asked.

I supposed Williams to be her husband.

" I thought you came from him."

I said, " Where am I going to sleep?"

She said, " There is a candle; you can go upstairs."

She made no movement to show me. I was therefore obliged to find my own quarters, and uncomfortable ones they were. I lay awake nearly the whole night. In the morning I went downstairs. I should say it wanted about two days to Christmas. I started off to find Mr. Burn, and saw on the road a decent-looking woman standing at the door of one of the houses, and I heard a man say to her, when I passed by, " There, that's him!"

He hailed and said, " How are you?"

" Not very well," I replied. " I have had a poor night's rest."

The wife said, " Come and look at the pigs. My husband was away from home six or seven weeks; but why," she added, turning to the man, " don't you tell the gentleman? Sir, he was arrested by you on the Seven Dials in London at a time when he had determined not to return home any more. He did, though, and now look at our little pigs."

"My very heart danced with joy at this incident. The rain and snow, the outside seat on the coach, the queer woman in the coffee-house, and the bad night I had passed, were alike forgotten; for here was an instance of the good effected by my instrumentality, which had turned up in the most unlikely place. I learned the full particulars. He had returned home, resolved to apply himself to work, and to adhere to teetotalism, and the result was seen in his happy home, in the comfortable appearance of himself and his wife, and, last of all, in his pigs.

The meeting was held in the Quakers' meeting-house, and Mr. Burn began to tell me what I was to say and what I was not to say. I listened attentively, and spoke to them as I always did. Five or six signed the pledge. This man (Andrews was his name) was present with his wife, and brought a good many with him. I have a book at home now which this grateful couple presented to me, entitled "Baxter's Alarm to Sinners."

The day after the meeting was Christmas. I said to Mr. Burn, "We have not had much success here, sir. When Christmas is over, I shall hold an open-air meeting under the Town Hall."

He said, "Thou must not do that."

"Why not?"

"Because it will cause an uproar."

"Uproar, or no uproar, I mean to hold the meeting."

And so I did. We commenced with the old hymn,—

"Rise and shine through every nation,
Oh thou Temperance star divine," &c.,

got five or six to sign the pledge, and not only that, but the teetotalers said, "We will have another meeting—a tea-meeting."

We had a tea-meeting, Tickets were bought and given away to some poor fellows who could not afford to pay. We had secured the schoolroom for the occasion, and a very comfortable party it was. We had a nice tea, and I sang them a song or two. In the midst of the meeting was a man who looked the wreck of a gentleman. He spoke to me, and said,—

"I heard you under the Town Hall, and if I could believe what you said, I would try to be a teetotaler."

"Why should you doubt what I said? What interest have I got in deceiving you? I have not come down here for yours, but for *you*, sir. Mr. Nettleton, the ironmonger in Chelsea, knows me, as does also Mr. Cubitt, the builder. I have been working for Mr. Cubitt for the last five or six years—in fact, nearly seven years, and you can write to any of them and ask them. What is the reason you should think I don't speak the truth?"

"Well, the fact is, that story about the oven gets over me. How could a man do what you describe yourself as having done?"

"A man, sir, can do almost anything if he tries."

By-and-by two or three got round me, and when this gentlemanly-looking fellow went to another part of the room they told me that he had married a minister's daughter, and he himself, it appears, was brought up to the ministry, but he fell away through drink; and on purpose to get his wife away from him, or rather from the misery she was enduring with him, her friends allowed him 1*l*. a week, and with this he could (after paying for the drink he consumed) just keep the clothes on his back. He was, it seems, a rare man for painting names for the farmers on carts, or over shop-doors.

"Where is his wife?" I asked, when the story was closed.

"She has gone home to her mother."

I then talked to him again, and gave him as much confidence as I could in his ability to keep the pledge. I wound up by telling him that he ought to sign it at once. He said,—

"I would if I thought I could keep it."

"You must try and keep it. You know the drink is your great curse, and what I want you to do is to flee from it. It cannot touch you, if you let it alone."

"Oh! there is not a word you have said but what I have felt—and felt keenly."

I could see by his appearance that he was eating the wormwood and drinking the gall of remorse. All the trouble he seemed to be in was to believe what I had said.

"You will never believe in me," I said, "until you have tried the medicine for yourself. When a man comes to Christ and feels he is a sinner, it is one of the hardest things in the world to believe that God gave His Son to die for him, because his sins seem so enormous, and the love seems so great—he thinks the news too good to be true, but yet for all that it is true. Now, you must try and believe what I say. I do not know what else I can say to you."

He shook hands very cordially with me, and I heard subsequently that he reformed, and that there was every prospect of his being united again to his wife.

Many more incidents of the work in Seven Dials, and elsewhere, might be given; but these are only selected from the number to show the power that teetotalism has (under the Divine blessing) in raising the most degraded and lost to positions of comfort and respectability.

ANNOUNCEMENTS OF MEETINGS.

A not uninteresting chapter in the future history of the temperance reformation will be that which is devoted to a description of the way in which the early meetings were convened. In the present "palmy days" the professional bill-poster does the work; but years ago, when funds were scarce, and friends still more so, the temperance reformer had to paste his own bills, or to act as his own bellman. Some quaint stories are told of the early temperance bill-posting. Mr. John Meredith used to go round with a gallipot of paste in one hand, a brush in the other, and some bills in his pocket in the small hours of the morning. On one of these expeditions he was nearly "run in" by an "active and intelligent officer," who could hardly credit Mr. Meredith's statement that he was out at that time in the morning "for the good of the cause."

Another story is told of Mr. Livesey, who, when he first visited London, was found posting small bills about the size of his hand inside the Bank of England! Mr. John Cassell used to take a big bell with him in the early days of our cause, and ring it in the towns to call the meeting together.

The religious bodies and the moderation society in the early days were very cool to us, if not actively against us. When we could not get a meeting-place anywhere else, we could generally get aid from the Primitive Methodists. The Rev. Hugh Bourne, one of their ministers, made many an effective speech for us. The Baptists, on the whole, treated us very well, but the Wesleyans would not open their doors to us. Thank God I have lived to see a Metropolitan Tabernacle demonstration on temperance under the sanction of the Conference itself. As for the Church of England, they thought it a sin to look at us. The Rev. W. W. Robinson, of Chelsea, was a notable exception to this rule.

OPEN-AIR MEETINGS—SUMMARY OF WORK.

SEVEN DIALS.—Meetings were held here under my superintendence for three and a half or four years every Sunday morning during the summer months. They were originated

SPITALFIELDS MARKET.—I had the pleasure in helping to originate these meetings with the kind help of some friends in Harp Alley. They were held only occasionally on Sunday afternoons and evenings. Altogether there must have been between twenty and twenty-five meetings each season.

SMITHFIELD MARKET.—I held meetings here every Sunday afternoon for two and a half years. Hundreds signed the pledge there. Mr. Green, Mr. Hatfield, Mr. Hart, Mr. Mathews, and others, were most willing assistants.

ISLINGTON GREEN.—I had the pleasure of originating the meetings held here on Sunday mornings. Several good friends, whose names I cannot remember, were at my back, and amongst them was Mr. Buteux and Mr. Joseph Leicester. The meetings were held, for a long time, every other Sunday, and they were continued after I had given them up.

CLERKENWELL GREEN.—I went to this place by myself, and originated my own meetings, although I believe there were meetings held there before. Mr. A. Brown, Mr. Thos. Hudson, Mr. Jabez Inwards, and the late Mr. George Howlett, Mr. George Aubrey, and Mr. Buteux stood by me in a right manly way. I believe Mr. A. Brown continues these meetings occasionally to this day.

KENNINGTON PARK.—Mr. Inwards and myself went here nearly every Sunday on horseback. The meetings lasted for two or three years, until the park was enclosed. The late George Howlett also assisted us.

LAMBETH WALK.—Mr. T. A. Smith and myself started these meetings, and well do I remember paying twopence for an orange-box to stand on. Mr. R. N. Bailey and Mr. McLachlan were active workers. These meetings were not continued very long by me.

THAMES BANK.—At these meetings, which were amongst the most successful held in London, nearly all the advocates attended. Amongst the principal were the Rev. S. Beardsall, Mr. Jabez Inwards, Mr. Thomas Whittaker, Mr. G. C. Campbell, Mr. J. T. Buteux, and Mr. Thomas Hudson. At that time my house was a house-of-call for them all. We had three meetings there; one at 11 a.m., one at 3 p.m., and another in the evening. They were continued for over five years, until the place got built upon. By this means we literally kept Chelsea alive on the subject of teetotal truth.

STARCH GREEN.—These meetings were started at the instigation of the late Mr. E. C. Tisdall, than whom there was not a harder worker in the temperance cause in England. He offered to give me a pony; for he said I should kill myself with so much walking. I should have gladly accepted the offer, only I had no place to keep it in.

JEWS' ROW, CHELSEA.—These were also some of my best meetings. They were continued for about eight years, and great good they did. It was at these meetings I used to be very greatly annoyed —— by a Mrs. L. She used to swear in the most dreadful way at me; but if anybody else did so, she would turn upon them like a tigress. In fact she considered it her exclusive privilege to abuse me.

Attending a meeting at Walworth some time after, who should come up to me but this self-same woman.

"God bless your beautiful (!) voice! I made up my mind to sign the pledge; and I said to my husband, 'If you don't come and sign the pledge along with me, I'll twist your neck;' and so we both signed together about a twelvemonth ago. We had attended the meetings in Kennington Park, and these are my two daughters. We sell ginger beer."

Eight or nine years afterwards I met her again, and asked how she was getting on. She said,—

"I saw in the papers that they wanted a man and his wife to look after these (Kennington Park) gardens, and I knew my L—— was a good gardener, so I went and asked them if they would take my husband; that he was a sober man, and that I was an industrious woman. They gave us the job, and here we have been ever since."

I called in to see the husband some five or six months later, and found him in a very bad way.

"I wanted to see you," he said, "very badly. I have lost my poor old girl; she is dead and buried. She died a teetotaler. The doctors wanted to persuade her out of it, but she would not listen to them. She was many years a faithful teetotaler, and was seventy-six when she died. They have never discharged me, and here I am still. The work has gone into the hands of a master gardener, but the company or the board keep me walking about just seeing that things are right. I have twenty-eight shillings a week, with a balance in the bank, and I am humbly thankful to God for all His mercies."

To resume, however. The Jews'-row meetings were originated by myself. Mr. Balfour, Mr. George Howlett, and nearly every one of those whom I have before mentioned, were of very great assistance to me. When the funds began to look up we got a movable platform, and I had the honour of first speaking from it. Mr. John Punch did me good service here and elsewhere. He stood by me and never flinched, even when I was marched to the station-house. Captain Newdon did the same, and for years and years they never missed a meeting at which I spoke. The meetings are held even now at the east end of the bridge by James Reynell, who is now a large cab proprietor, but who at one time was only a bricklayer's labourer. Such is the power of teetotalism to raise in the social scale all classes of men.

NEW BRIDGE.—The meetings have been continued here or at the "White Stiles" ever since 1837. The principal facts in connexion with them have already been given.

WORKING MEN'S HALL, LOWER GEORGE-STREET, CHELSEA.—This hall has done service of a very essential kind to the temperance cause. It still remains, and I hope ever will remain, as a monument of perseverance, faith, and energy of the early temperance workers. Mr. Johnson, Mr. Dyke, and Mr. James Reynell attend there every Sunday night. If my good old friend, Mr. Reynell, knows I am going to a meeting, he will take his cab to drive me to it. The George-street Hall has been open for nearly twenty-eight years.

WESTMINSTER PUMP.—Torrents of teetotal advocacy have poured forth from this place. I was often called the "Westminster Pump." Mr. Punch relieved me here, so that I was able to go and break ground in other directions; but not until I had been pouring away there for a period of fifteen years.

There were many other meetings which I occasionally attended, such as those at the Duke of York's Column and elsewhere; but the foregoing are mostly meetings which I originated, carried on for a time, and then handed over to workers in the locality.

THE OLD TEMPERANCE HYMNS.

The aid that singing has been to the higher cause of religion is only surpassed by that which it has been to the temperance cause. All our meetings, without exception, were opened at least with singing, if not with prayer. The hymns used were those composed by our good old friend the Rev. S. Beardsall, of sainted memory. Some of them remain to this day.

CHAPTER VI.

FIRST STEPS TOWARDS INDEPENDENCE IN WORLDLY CIRCUM-STANCES.—SABBATH CONVICTIONS.

THERE is a very noble verse of my countryman, Robert Burns, which I have ever heard with admiration:—

> "To catch Dame Fortune's golden smile,
>   Assiduous wait upon her,
> And gather gear by every wile
>   That's justified by honour.
> Not for to hide it in a hedge,
>   Not for a train attendant,
> But for the glorious privilege
>   Of being independent."

That motive seems to me to be right for both worlds. Honest independence leads to true Christian manliness.

THE BUILDING AND SALE OF MY FIRST HOUSE.

When I left working at Her Majesty's Palace,[1] I, under the circumstances mentioned elsewhere, had arrived at a turning-point in my worldly fortunes. Shakespeare has said that "There is a tide in the affairs of men, which taken at the flood

---

[1] See p. 80.

leads on to fortune;" and I believe the tide of my fortunes came at this time; and, through the blessing of God, it *was* taken at the flood. If it has not led me on to fortune, it has at least led me to a position of comfort and respectability, which at one period of my life I would have deemed it impossible for me by any amount of diligence to attain. I was without work and without friends, though, thanks to teetotalism, I had a little money deposited in a place where I could easily get it—the Savings' Bank at Chelsea. It was in the year 1840 that I went to see Mr. Thomas Cubitt, whom I desire to mention with gratitude and respect. I told him my circumstances, and that I wanted to build a house.

"Well," he said, "take a piece of ground for half-a-dozen houses."

"I am frightened to go too far at first," I replied.

"Very well," he said, "there is nothing like making sure steps. You are our temperance man," he added; "I remember you well."

This was the commencement of my rise in the world above the position of a common journeyman. Mr. Cubitt offered me bricks upon credit sufficient to get the roof on, if I could find money for the rest. I had 65*l*. of my own—the savings of three years' teetotalism—and to work I went, and soon got the skeleton of the house up on the piece of ground he granted in Wellington-street, Pimlico. Although I used to rise with the lark I was nevertheless at a teetotal meeting every night, while on Sunday I was lecturing all day long. I would not give up my temperance work for any man or anything. My son and myself used to get up at four o'clock in the morning, and make up a batch of mortar, so as to be ready to set the labourers to work when they came. We had two labourers to assist us, and now and then I took on a man just to give him a little help to tide over the hard time immediately succeeding his signing the pledge. At times I used to go away, and perhaps my son with me, to another job, which would bring in a little money. When I got the roof on I was in a terrible fix. I had spent all my money, and though Mr. Cubitt was ready to give me all I wanted, yet I did not know him as I do now. I got into very low spirits, but as in leaving her Majesty's Palace I had made that a matter of prayer, so also did I do with this. My wife also prayed, and thus the matter was left *apparently* no better than before.

One day I went down to my work as usual, and on looking up the street, which was then beginning to form, I saw Mr. Robert Alsop[1] coming along—the very man who brought two policemen to take me in charge for holding meetings at the "White Stiles," Chelsea. He did this perhaps partly on his own account, and partly because the people sent a petition to have me removed from the spot. It may be as well to give a little account of what transpired when Mr. Alsop brought the two policemen.[2]

"I give," he said, "this man in charge. I have told him that the people about here are much offended. We cannot allow this disturbance to go on, and a letter has been sent on the subject. I therefore give him in charge."

"Then," said I, "I give Mr. Alsop in charge, and I dare you to take me without taking him."

The policemen were in a fog—likewise Mr. Alsop.

"Well, sir," said one of them at last, "it appears Mr. McCurrey knows what he is doing. We know nothing about

---

[1] Mr. Alsop was a teetotaler from 1837.

[2] Mr. Alsop was always a great friend to the temperance cause, but he feared that open-air advocacy might lead to rioting; and, as a lover of peace and order, he, *for a time*, disapproved of out-door gatherings. This explains the reason of a temporary misunderstanding. In all plans to do good there is room for different modes of operation.—[*Ed. of MSS.*]

the case, and if you force us to take this man in charge we must take you too."

Mr. Alsop considered for a little. He did not know what to do. The people and the policemen were alike awaiting his decision. If he persisted, he must be conveyed like a culprit along with me; and he knew well that I cared little what was done, for by this time the roads to the various station-houses were getting pretty familiar. If, on the contrary, he retired from the conflict, he must do so with the ridicule of all about him. I think he chose the wisest course. He walked away amidst the derisive laughter of the crowd.

This then was the man whom God, and God alone, had sent to relieve me from my embarrassment. I stood in front of the house as Mr. Alsop came by, thinking what on earth I should do, but never for a moment dreaming that he was likely to be a customer.

"What will be the amount?" said Mr. Alsop, pausing in his walk, and looking up at the house.

I said, "When it is finished, and you have a good tenant, I will sell it to you for 380*l.* It has sixteen feet frontage, and is twenty-six feet deep."

"Who is the tenant to be?"

"I will be your tenant. I will take it for five or seven years."

"Well, I will think of it. I will call and see thee to-morrow."

As usual I made it a matter of prayer. The reader may be sure that I kept a good look-out for my customer the next day, but did not let *him* see that I was at all anxious about the matter.

"Have you thought about what I said?"

God knows I had not slept for thinking of it.

"Yes, I have, and I will take 380*l.* for it, and be your tenant for three, five, or seven years. I am going to leave my present house."

"I will give you 330*l*.," he said.

"Very well, I will take that. You know it is usual to pay a deposit."

"Oh! yes; how much do you want? I have brought a blank cheque."

"150*l*. would be enough.

"You can have more—say 200*l*."

"Very well—that will do."

He filled up the cheque for the last-mentioned amount, and we parted for the time. I was in the highest spirits. My difficulties had vanished. With this cheque I could command all the remaining materials I wanted. I went to Mr. Cubitt's office, got the boards for the floor, and everything else, and set the carpenters to work early and late. At last it was finished. Before this, however, I took ground for two more houses, which Mr. Alsop also bought. The first one I lived in myself for seven years. This was the very man who had given me in charge not nine months before.

I went on building and building until I gave up taking ground for one or two houses, but took it for ten, then fifteen, then twenty, and then for twenty-seven. All one side of Bessborough-street was built by me. My son was an immense help to me. Of course, as might have been expected, my career was not one of uninterrupted prosperity. Things went very hard with me once or twice, but my troubles were chiefly owing to the political commotion of the times, which disturbed trade and unsettled men's minds. The Chartist riots did me some harm, as did also the Feargus O'Connor disturbances and some trade disputes.

It was during the time of the Chartist disturbances that my troubles reached their climax, and that I really thought that the results for which I had so long laboured were about to be removed from my reach for ever. One day, when I was really unable to say how my engagements were to be met, one of my foremen came and said there was a gentleman wanting to see me about a house. I said,—

"Don't bother! no one wants to buy a house in these times."

"But he is a decent-looking man," said the foreman.

"It's no good. I see no hope of getting out of the present difficulties, and I shall have to discharge you all."

"I advise you to see him. He looks a business man."

I went to see the gentleman, who was no other than the father of Dr. Moore. As it happened, this was another turning-point in my life.

"What do you want for this house?"

"Seven hundred guineas."

"Well, I will come and look at it on Sunday with my son."

"I can't show it to you then. I don't do business on Sunday."

"Very well, I don't know that I can come again."

The next day, which was Sunday, passed in a very uncomfortable manner. Listening to the sermon even, the thought flashed before me as to whether I had not better have made the appointment, but it was dismissed at once. I was almost glad when the Sunday went over. The next day I really had an impression that he would come, and I said so to my wife. She agreed with me.

At half-past ten that morning, to my great delight, the 'bus stopped at the corner of the street, and the young Doctor and his father alighted.

"I have told my son," said the old Doctor, "that you wouldn't let us see your house on the Sunday, and we both say you did quite right. If a man can't do without working on

Sunday, he will never do with it. I went to sea when I was fourteen years of age, and have travelled the world almost twice over, and I have done my business without working on Sunday."

He looked at the house, and liked it very well, and then said,—

"I will give you the money in Dutch Consols."

"Well, Doctor, I don't know what Dutch Consols. really are; I want seven hundred guineas in British money."

He left me, the matter being still rather uncertain; but the next day he came to see me again, and I took him into my parlour. He said,—

"I have the money ready—50*l.*—for a deposit. I have brought it in money, as perhaps you will like it better that way."

"Thank you; I will give you a receipt."

"No," he said, "you needn't. I know your countrymen are a respectable, honest lot but for the drink, and I know you will not want to be paid twice."

The business was settled, and a friendship sprang up between myself and the old gentleman which lasted until he died. The arrangements for his funeral were entrusted to me, and were carried out without any of the men employed being allowed to partake of intoxicating drinks. In this way those disgraceful scenes which so frequently are associated with funerals were altogether avoided, and I was subsequently complimented by Dr. Moore, jun., on the highly respectable way in which the arrangements were carried out.

THOUGHTS ON THE SABBATH.

I was sometimes (as I have before said) reproached for speaking in the open air on the Sabbath-day, but my love for the blessings of that day was increased when I found I was able to do the Lord's work, and enlarge His kingdom. I felt myself employed as a scout to gather to the camp the deserters from the army of the Lord. But this made me very jealous that I did not do my own work on that day, or let worldly care encroach upon it. Indeed, I felt afraid that even using ordinary means of saving myself from extra toil on that day might cause my good to be evil spoken of. I may name an incident at

KINGSDOWN.

I received an invitation from a Baptist minister in this place (which is a little below Dartford) to speak upon the temperance question. I could not get away very well on Saturday, so I resolved (against my wife's advice) to go on the Sunday morning. When I arrived, the Baptist minister and his family were at family prayer. When I went to speak, I could hardly utter a word. The conviction was strong on my mind that I had not done right in coming there on Sunday. The lecturer who was with me asked what on earth was the matter. I told him, and he said, "If you are so tender, you should not have come down on the Sunday." After the morning's effort I went off in a private place by myself, and, taking my hat off, I asked God to have mercy upon me, and remove the awful load that was at my heart. Coming home I got into the train; and on the North Kent Line, as many of my readers know, there is the Blackheath Tunnel, which, I think, is said to be a mile and a quarter in length. Through some cause or other the train was stopped in the middle of the tunnel, and then occurred a scene which could only be rivalled in the bottomless pit. Women were screaming, and men were shouting and swearing in the most dreadful way, and there was I with all the feelings of the Prodigal in the strange country. That occurred twenty years ago, and since then I have never travelled on a Sunday—not even by an omnibus, except once only in Birmingham.

HER MAJESTY'S PALACE.

I was one of those employed on this important structure. I very frequently used to be working for the Baroness Burdett Coutts, Lord Paget, and others in the same rank of life. When I was at work one Saturday, some one came in and said that her Majesty was expected home, and that the apartments which she occupied must be finished by a certain time that was named. And in order to get them done by the appointed time, my employer, a Mr. Evans, said I must work all Sunday. I said,—

"I will not work at all on Sunday, though I am prepared to work till midnight every other day to get the work done, or I am willing to come at two o'clock in the morning on Monday, and work till it is finished."

He said, "You are not a loyal subject."

"Yes, I am; and if anybody were to tell me the palace was on fire, and her Majesty inside, I would risk my life to save her; but I won't risk my soul, for the sake of working on Sundays."

The consequence of all this was that I got my discharge, and from that moment I began to get on, on my own account. This was one of God's blessings in disguise. When I came home my wife said,—

"Never mind about it;" and we kneeled down and prayed, and we opened the hymn-book at the very hymn where it says,—

> "Ye fearful saints, fresh courage take,
> The clouds ye so much dread
> Are big with mercy, and shall break
> In blessings on your head."

I was really encouraged by this. It seemed like the omen of mercy and goodness, which has ever since followed me in my path through life.

CHAPTER VII.

SAD RECORDS OF THE VICTIMS.—WARNINGS.

THE incidents that I have known of accidents of violent death through strong drink would fill volumes. Some foolish, superstitious, and reckless sayings among the working-classes, have a tendency to perpetuate either utter carelessness or impious presumption. They will say, "Oh, drunken men and children are always preserved." Indeed, I have heard them say, "Well, Providence is very good to the poor fellows that take a drop too much;" and some have a kind of devil-trust— I may say worship. "Sure, the devil takes care of his own!" was a common cry in Seven Dials.

I was as reckless as the rest in my old days of intemperance, yet, blessed be God, my mother's teaching so far clung to me that in my worst days I felt that I did not deserve to escape, and that if I had been cut off God would have been just.

I remember a

TERRIBLE ACCIDENT THROUGH STRONG DRINK AND THE DRINKING CUSTOMS.

Two or three doors from where Mr. Hammond now has his Good Templar Depôt, I once had a job to do for a Mr.

Brunel—not the great engineer. He was himself working at it, and one day one of the labourers was three parts drunk, owing to a bad practice of giving them the old wood. I told him to mind what he was about, and not to venture up the ladder, but he did. He climbed to the top of the house holding the guide-rope, and fell from thence to the ground. The blood gushed out of his mouth, nose, and ears, and when raised he was dead!

As I read in the papers the many accidents that occur at chemists' shops by the shopmen selling wrong medicines or sending wrongly made up prescriptions, I feel that it is wonderful more cases do not happen. Among many others, I recollect vividly the case of a

CHEMIST'S ASSISTANT.

I once was asked to go to a very nice young fellow, an assistant in a chemist's shop. He was under the influence of drink when I arrived. I asked him how he felt. He described very accurately what his state was. He said that the appetite for drink came on him like a fit, and he added,—

"There is no bottle in this shop containing spirits but what I have drained it dry."

I talked very quietly, but very pointedly to him. I showed him that teetotalism was his only earthly hope in overcoming this evil, and I left him fully resolved to abide by the pledge, which I persuaded him to take. He stuck to it very firmly for about a month, and then he broke out. We saved him from destruction once more. We read the Scriptures to and prayed with him. His father was a minister in the country, and came up to London with some friends to see him, and to see the sights which our great city presents. Drink was taken in the course of their ramblings, and the poor fellow found himself locked up in the station-house. It preyed very much upon his mind, for he said, "I am ruined and disgraced now for ever." I did all I could to get him to sign the pledge again. That very afternoon he managed to elude his keepers, for he was under *delirium tremens*. He secretly crossed the road, and took a room in a coffee-house. He never rested that night, and in the morning his landlady was very much troubled, as also was the keeper of the coffee-house, for he had not heard his lodger move during the night. The former came round to see me about him, and having traced him to the coffee-house we went there, burst open his door, and beheld a most pitiable sight. He was lying dead upon the bed, having poisoned himself with oil of almonds, which he had taken from his own shop.

I often wonder that self-interest, if no higher motive, does not make the sober part of the community desire the spread of temperance principles.

JOHN CLARK.

John C—— was a relation of my first wife's, and we were both brought up together as young men. When he came to London he went to work as a dentist for a Mr. Cartwright, and got on very well indeed; so much so, that at one stretch his wages were advanced from 200*l*. to 350*l*. a year. His wife and himself were about as creditable people as you could find anywhere. Money was plentiful, and perhaps that had something to do with his end. He went into business for himself near Russell-square. He succeeded so well there, that he moved into a larger house himself, though he still retained the other. But he soon carried on "glorification" at somebody else's expense. Some fellows of the "jolly" sort assembled, and ordered a large crate of wine. Three months after a bill was sent in for this wine. C—— declared he never bought it, and the senders as stoutly declared that it was delivered at his house. They employed a lawyer, and he employed a lawyer; and that circumstance, trifling as it appeared, was the means of breaking up his business, and bringing on his death. He was turned out of house and home through the expenses he was put to, aided by his drinking habits; and the policy for which his life was insured, amounting to 2000*l.*, lapsed in consequence of his forgetting to keep up the payments. He died in an arm-chair at his residence in Edgware-road, in a most miserable condition. He was a man of talent, who might have made his way (and did make it so far as he left the drink alone) in the world; but the drink, which strikes down the great and the mighty, struck him down. When he died, his two daughters were left penniless. Their uncle Ebenezer took them. That was twenty years ago. He was doing well then, but he too has since fallen by drink, and all he now has to live on is what he gets from me. As an instance of the way in which people cling to the intoxicating cup, I may mention that these two daughters are not teetotalers; though by way of warning to them I once, and only once, reminded them of the melancholy end of their father and mother, of what they were doing, and as to the consequences which were likely to ensue. They laughed the matter off. My poor relative very soon got turned out of his house, and is now a most miserable fellow, quite dependent on me. I have done all I could to put him right again, but it is of no avail. I got a letter to say, "If you don't come down and see C——, he will be locked up in Lewes Gaol. He has been setting fire to the house of a person with whom he has been living." I went down, but he was in Lewes Gaol when I arrived. The woman who was living next door told me the circumstances. He appears to have got newspapers, sheets, and everything that he could lay his hands on, put them in the middle of the room, bolted the door, and set fire to them. He then sat upon the sofa, and laughed like a maniac at the destruction he was causing. The door was burst open, and he was thus saved from being burnt to death, and the house from utter destruction. I was led through the room, and there was the place in the middle, to which the fire had been confined, charred as black as a cinder.

"Merciful me!" I cried, "how did he do this?"

I was then told that one Sandy McLaughlin, who was his boon companion, and had been drinking with him at the time, could give me an explanation. He didn't tell me much about the matter—in fact, I found he was drunk!

THE CASE OF MRS. CURTIS.

The "Pump" at Westminster will be remembered by many poor reclaimed inebriates until their dying day. The meetings held there have been the means of reclaiming hundreds. Our present Grand Worthy Secretary of the Independent Order of Good Templars was convinced there. He was led to think first there, and after at the Thames Bank. The Rev. Robert Maguire, M.A., now the much-respected Rector of St. Olave's, once in a public meeting dated his conversion to teetotalism to me.

Two weeks (or it might only have been one) after I had addressed the meeting at the Pump about twenty-eight years ago, a lady came to my house and knocked at the door. There was a bill in the window:—" Front and back parlour to let." I was at that time on my own account, and sported a zinc plate on my door, which informed the public that the occupant of the house was—

"J. McCurrey, bricklayer and whitewasher. Scullery stoves and ranges set in the best manner and on the most reasonable terms."

Mrs. Curtis came in to inquire after the apartments, and my wife told her that the rent was 6s. 6d. She said,—

"I want to ask you a question. Is the gentleman's name

who is on the door that of the gentleman who talks about temperance and speaks all over London? I ask because I have heard him at 'Westminster Pump.'"

My wife said I was the man.

"Well, then, I will take the lodgings."

She left a small deposit, as was the custom, and on the following Tuesday came to take possession, bringing with her a van-load of goods of a rather superior description. We were very glad of this, for it was a kind of guarantee that we had a respectable tenant. She lived there about a week or ten days without seeing me. We were then living in the kitchen, for this was the first house I took, but we soon moved into parlours. I was rather curious to see her, she having inquired so about me. I watched my opportunity, and one Sunday morning, as she was going out, I came up just in time to wish her good morning. She replied, "Good morning."

"My wife was saying that I know you, but I don't."

The result of the conversation that ensued was that she came in to breakfast with us at my invitation. My boys and girls sung some hymns, and I had family prayer. I got an opportunity of pouring out my soul fully when on my knees. After prayers we became quite friendly. I asked her where her husband was, and she replied that he was a traveller, and that he never came home much. She told us she was going to see her doctor, who ordered her wine. I said to her,—

"I am afraid the doctor is too free with his wine orders, and he is giving you too much."

"I take it because he says it will do me good."

"Well, I don't think it will do much good to a woman in the sad condition you are in."

She was evidently in a consumption.

I resolved subsequently to speak to her doctor, and asked

him how he thought she was getting on, and he said he thought she was sinking.

"What do you give her so much drink for? She is half stupid now, and I don't believe she requires such things as that at all. She requires something soothing."

A rather warm conversation ensued, but she got no more alcohol from the doctor. The disease rapidly gained upon her; and when she felt that her time was drawing short, she unfolded to me the story of her life. It was a melancholy record. Decoyed away from home by the false promises of a monster—I cannot call him a man—she had led an immoral life for many years, and was first led to think of the better way when she heard me at the Pump. She said now to my wife,—

"God will bless you and your husband for your kindness to me. I just want to make one request: will you let me hold your hands until I die?"

I said, "Oh, yes." She caught hold of our two hands, and in this position she was when the doctor came. I told him in a whisper what was her state, and he said, "She is not far off." About half an hour before she died she rallied and said,—

"I am thinking about my mother. I shall soon see my mother. I broke my mother's heart, and my father didn't know where I was. You will find a letter in my box, which you will open and send."

> "Oh! to grace, how great a debtor,
>   Daily I'm constrain'd to be;
> Let Thy love now like a fetter,
>   Bind my wandering heart to Thee."

In about another ten minutes or a quarter of an hour she said,—

"I'm going to see my Saviour," and fell back in bed and died.

MR. BARNES.

Mr. Barnes was the son of a doctor, who left, besides him, two other sons and two daughters. Mr. Barnes was taken into Cubitt's establishment, and he turned out one of the cleverest of the men there. But he gave way to drunkenness, and at the request of Mr. Cubitt's nephew I did my utmost to get him to sign the pledge. He did so, and kept it for a fortnight or three weeks. He took some land on which to build before this, but all through drink became a bankrupt. At last two men were kept in his room to watch him, and under these circumstances only, he resisted the raging appetite which was within him. Just at that time Mr. Thomas Cubitt died, and Mr. Barnes left the establishment at the age of about twenty-four or twenty-five, and under the Commissioners of Woods and Forests obtained a situation of about 250*l.* a year to begin with. The way he behaved there in consequence of drink was such that he was discharged never to return. Thus he was thrown into poverty with his wife, who was a gentleman's daughter. He again signed the pledge in my house, and commenced business for himself once more. There was no doubt but that he was on the road to success again, but once more the drink demon showed his fangs, but this time in a new form. His wife took drink, and I saw her in a sad condition with my poor friend. When I made some remark to her about her folly, she uttered a sentence which I have never forgotten. She said,—

"I can be a teetotaler fast enough if I like, but I drink more now, because I don't want Henry to drink so much."

The remark was a curious one, and whether there is any philosophy in it I will leave the reader to judge. In spite of this shock he went on very well for a twelvemonth. He took ground at Brixton which had about eight or nine feet of gravel, or sand, all over it. That alone paid for the first story of his houses, and he was prospering. Unfortunately his wife still continued her drinking ways, and he began to swear the most dreadful things concerning her. He returned to drink, and as he did so his property began to disappear like the mist. In the midst of this he suddenly went to his account. The wife came to me when he was dead with a very pitiful story.

"Don't come to me," I said to her, with a feeling of contempt which I took no pains to conceal. "Don't come to me. You never acted the part of a true wife to your husband, or he would have been alive now. Let me know how he died."

"He came home and said he was not well, and said he wanted some pills to make him better."

"You have been drinking to-day, woman," I said, as the odious smell reached my nostrils.

"I have only had a little drop of beer. I went to the doctor," she continued, "to tell him to come and see him, and when I came back with the medicine he was dead."

This was the end of Mr. Barnes. He died before he had reached the prime of life, and with talents which might have adorned any profession.

JOHN MARSDEN.

John Marsden was a carpenter, and a better tradesman never handled a tool. He was a poor dissipated fellow when I first got hold of him, and, of course, he was very hard up. Good wages are of no earthly use to a man who spends them recklessly in drink. He came and asked me for a job. I did find him one in Aldersgate-street, and having signed the pledge he became a most useful fellow. He got on very well indeed, and his wife was an industrious woman. He took it into his head to start in business on his own account. I said,—

"Stop where you are, if you take my advice."

"No, I won't, I mean to have a horse to ride on."

"What do you want with a horse?"

"Never mind; I mean to have one."

He commenced in business for himself, and broke his pledge six months afterwards. He went from bad to worse, until the difficulty was to find him sober. He got a horse (though where from I don't know), and came round to see me.

"Didn't I tell you I should have a nice mare?" he said, driving up and down to show me how well he could ride, as his horse cantered. Poor fellow! he looked very well then, but how did he look a very short time after, when he came to see me once more—a paralytic? Ah! How! He was only able to stand by leaning against the wall. He could hardly speak.

"Where is your wife?" I asked.

"I don't know."

"Where have you been yourself?"

"I have just come out of the hospital to-day."

"Ah! my friend, it wants more than the help of man to hold to this pledge: it wants the help of God."

I helped him as far as I could, but shortly after he died, was buried by the workhouse, and his wife and children were left destitute.

MR. M———S.

Mr. M———s was head manager for an eminent firm of civil engineers in Parliament-street, Westminster. He bought a house from me, and arrangements were made for the money to be paid at the solicitor's office.

"Come, McCurrey," he said, "we mustn't have this a dry job. Let's have a glass of wine."

I refused, and dropped a word of warning into his ear, which he passed by unheeded. He sent for the wine and some biscuits, he filled up the glass, and offered it to me. I again declined; whereupon he swore that if I didn't drink he would not have the house.

"Oh! in that case there is no harm done. You pay the solicitor what he has done for you. I have got your deposit in my pocket, and here it is for you."

He paid for the house, and subsequently sent for me and apologized for the way he had spoken when settling for it. On leaving him, he said,—

"Here is a bottle of good old port, take it home to Mrs. McCurrey. I said, in joke,—

"Do you want me to get my hair combed with the poker? or my skull cracked?"

He never offered me drink any more, but when he died the property he left was all squandered by his second wife, and the children were left at the mercy of the world.

HUTCHINSON, THE GUNSMITH.

Mr. Hutchinson, whom I knew, was one of the best gunsmiths in England, but he was much given to drink. He used to lounge, and drink and smoke. On one occasion he set fire to the house. He got very heavily into my debt, and though even his wife urged me to sell the things and pay myself I refused to do so. He promised over and over again to do better, but in vain. I got him to be a teetotaler for three or four months, and during that time he could get as much as thirty or forty guineas for a gun. One day he came to me, and with a dreadful oath said,—

"What do you think of my sister? she's burnt me out with a candle. The smell came up through the house, and the policeman knocked at the door; and when they got out the fire, they found my sister burnt to death."

I went to ascertain the truth of this terrible story. I found the house shut up, and a policeman guarding the door. He told me that it was true enough. He said it was a mercy that he came past, or the brother and another sister would have been burnt as well. They were all sitting there drinking at the time. What Hutchinson is doing now, or where he is, I cannot say, for I have not seen him for years.

ROSSITER.

Rossiter's father was the head carman for the Equitable Gas Works, and, in fact, the Company had such confidence in him that there was nothing done by anybody else that could be done by him. When he died there was nothing more natural than that his son should be appointed to succeed him, and there is no doubt he might have done as well as his father but for the drink. I caught him once or twice very nearly setting fire to my place when he was in his drunken fits. At last I was obliged to tell him to leave my stable altogether. His horse died, and his cart was sold by himself for 5*l.* or 6*l.* He then thoroughly gave way to drunken habits, and died shortly after. This is an instance of how the drink works in a different way with different people. The father appears to have been a steady-going moderate drinker, and to have lived and died as such all his life. The son attempts to follow in the father's footsteps and fails most miserably, and at an early age descends into a dishonoured grave. It is for moderate drinkers to answer as best they can the question, "Is it wise and safe to drink?"

HARRY FORD.

Harry Ford worked with me at Cubitt's when I was a journeyman. He was literally ruined through having 800*l.* left him. After he had spent his money like the Prodigal, and had become reduced to the Prodigal's poverty, he came to work in the Chalk Farm Tunnel, which was then being constructed, and the very worst place he could have come to. It was the most drunken place I ever saw. There was a certain kind of stuff underneath, which was of such value that he could sell it for beer. The work was divided into shifts of 4s. 6d. each, and by working hard we could make three shifts in two days, which would be 13s. 6d. The poor fellow had become so debilitated by the results of long debauchery, that when he came up to have his breakfast between four and five one morning he laid down on the settle and never rose any more. At his funeral a lot of bricklayers were present, and they actually took with them a bottle of gin, and drank it over his grave, shouting as they did, that he was a "jolly good fellow." After this took place his son used occasionally to come to our Teetotal Hall, but his wife was not a hair's-breadth better than the man who thus died. We had a large concert one night in the Lower Hall, George-street, and this son saw Mr. Johnson, our Secretary, counting the money and putting it in his pocket. This young fellow, with some more of the same sort, made a most desperate and brutal assault in the passage; but they mistook their man in the dark, and nearly killed one of our members. They used the instruments called "knuckle-dusters," and most fearful were the injuries they inflicted with them upon our poor member—injuries which disfigured him for life. On the day when the villain was tried, our member was able to be in the witness-box to identify him. The result was that he was sentenced to penal servitude for fourteen years.

MR. LOCKE.

I knew Mr. Locke when he was a boy. He had highly respectable parents, and was learning to be a mason with a man of the name of Lowrie, who was a master mason now some forty years ago. When I renewed my acquaintance with him in London, he was a first-class foreman in Cubitt's. He was most invaluable to the firm. By the very ring of the marble he could tell its quality, and cleared for Mr. Cubitt (as that gentleman himself was not slow to admit) many a 1000*l*. Mr. Cubitt thought so much of him that he allowed him a nice brougham and horse, and a man to drive him; so that Mr. Locke became quite a gentleman. Just in proportion as he prospered, just in that proportion did the drink unman him. He was forgiven again and again for his drunkenness, and, of course, in the case of a man with such an income as he had, there were many who were watching, only too ready to profit by his misfortunes. On one occasion, when he was unable to step out of his brougham through sheer drunkenness, he insulted Mr. Cubitt, and was discharged off the premises. Two years later I saw him in the Clock Tower of the Houses of Parliament, when the building of that remarkable structure was going on. He recognized me, and he must have seen how truly grieved I felt for him in the position to which he had reduced himself. I talked very kindly and very respectfully to him, to get him to sign the pledge. It was not long afterwards that he died in the midst of the greatest poverty.

GURLING.

Mr. Gurling was a pork-butcher, and was highly successful in business. Early and late he was at it, but he too was another of those who seemed to be ruined by prosperity. He began to get very fond of drink. I became acquainted mainly through his being at the Great Hall, Westminster, and through my own desire, because I saw what a clean and industrious fellow he was. I could not fail to observe the predilection he showed for drink, and I spoke to him about it. He made me the same kind of off-hand reply that Locke had done, and so things went on. One morning my son came running in, and said,—

"Father, Mr. Gurling is out in the middle of the road, and tearing his handkerchief over the railings all to pieces. He is swearing at the people in the other house, and saying that they have taken away his cash-box."

I ran out and spoke to him. He neither knew nor spoke to me, and we were obliged to take him off to the hospital, and there he died. After his death the pork-shop went to ruin. This man was two years and a half Secretary to the Great Hall in Westminster, and for that time was a stanch teetotaler. Had he remained in that position, there is every reason to believe that for years and years he would have lived a sober and useful man.

DANIEL GOODE.

Daniel Goode, whose career is, alas! to be found recorded in the annals of the Newgate Calendar, was a teetotaler for nearly two years and a half. We called him "Blueskin," on account of the peculiar waistcoats he used to wear. He had been a coachman, but was discharged from his employment through drink. He was recommended by an Irish gentleman to Mr. Thomas Cubitt, who employed him for two years; and during that time I got him to become a teetotaler. After he had been with Mr. Cubitt the time already mentioned, he went to Larkhall-lane to apply for a situation as coachman. He succeeded. Of course he was at once placed in the midst of temptation, but he seemed awhile to have refrained from yielding to it. He used to call round on me on horseback. On one occasion I said I was not quite sure of his teetotalism. He laughed it off, but I was glad I said it, to let him see that I was suspicious of him. I did not see him for a long time, but at last the awful deed he did came out. He murdered the woman with whom he was living, and burnt her body piece by piece in the harness-room, and got rid of all but her trunk, which was under the manger of the stable. There was a dreadful smell, and the inquiries which were made as to the cause of it discovered the awful secret. Some of the men in Cubitt's told Goode more than once that he had the gallows in his face. Little did they think how true their words were. We need not go into the horrible tale; and those who wish to do so (if there are any), can find them in the choice publication I have before mentioned. On seeing that his discovery was inevitable, he managed to escape. A reward of 150*l.* was offered for his apprehension. One of the men whom I knew well as a workman in Cubitt's, named Bill Rosier, and who happened to be working at Cubitt's, met and recognized him in spite of his false name. He mentioned the circumstance to his master, who, unknown to Goode, sent for a couple of policemen. Goode was arrested, tried, condemned, and executed at the Old Bailey, and his body given over for dissection.

THOMAS WOODCOCK.

Thomas Woodcock was a member of the Wesleyan Methodist Society and a class-leader. He was very strongly opposed to the temperance movement. He would never recognize the principle of abstinence from strong drink as a true one at all. Alas! poor fellow, he disappeared from that religious body in a cloud of shame. I found him in a workhouse, and, to use the words I expressed to James Reynell, when speaking to that good friend on the subject,—

"He is a poor broken-down, miserable man in the Chelsea Workhouse, but he is a man who, nevertheless, might have been a happy, respectable, and well-to-do man, if he had only left the accursed drink alone."

I am sorry to say that it has not unfrequently been my lot to see the bitterest opponents of the temperance movement brought, in their own individual cases, to feel the terrible force of a raging appetite, and the awfully seductive influence of the demon drink. Were a collection made of such cases, it would be one of the most startling chapters in the altogether startling story of the deeds of intemperance.

MR. STEWART.

It was my lot to become acquainted with a Mr. Stewart, a corn-merchant. He was a well-to-do man, but he drank very heavily. One day I said to him,—

"When are you going to leave off the drink?"

He said, "I don't know."

"You are looking very sadly," and so indeed he was. Within a week of that short conversation, he died suddenly of *delirium tremens*.

JACK HALL.

I was not a teetotaler when I became acquainted with this man. We were working quite close to the "White Horse" public-house in the Theobald's-road, Holborn. We were all drinking together in the fore-part of the day, resolving to go to work after dinner. Hall, in stumbling out of the public-house, fell upon the kerb-stone, and actually split open his breast. We picked him up, and put him into a kind of carpenter's shop that was near. When he lay there under the cold hand of death, I declare I never saw a man look more the picture of life. Though a warning like this even did not produce any very lasting impression, it made a salutary one for the time being.

MR. WATSON.

Mr. Watson, a Scotchman by birth, was first employed in

Mr. Thomas Cubitt's as an engineer. He remained there two years, and was very highly respected. He left that, and shortly after, by Mr. Cubitt's recommendation, was made manager of the London Gas Works in the room of the former manager, who was drowned whilst on his way to the Isle of Wight—the small boat in which he was a passenger being upset by the swell of a steamer. Just as prosperity began to smile on Watson, the cloven foot of the old enemy began to appear. Often have I said to him,—

"Why don't you give up the drink? Mind my word, if you don't, it will be the death of you."

"Do you think I am a drunkard?"

I was silent. It would not do to tell him the candid opinion I had already more than half formed. I, however, said,—

"You are a local preacher, Mr. Watson, of the Methodist New Connexion, and you ought certainly to set a better example than you do."

He made very little remark about it. He perished shortly after, raving mad through drink, and his wife died of a broken heart.

WILLIAM BENNETT AND OTHERS.

Abstainers are frequently charged with exaggerating the evils of intemperance. Before I became a teetotaler I was once in a public-house in Lisson-grove, where, in consequence of a drunken brawl, a fight ensued, and one of the men at the very outset was killed on the spot. William Bennett was the name of the man who struck the blow, but the jury having brought in a verdict of manslaughter, he was only sentenced to twelve months' imprisonment.

In another case, which I knew well enough, a bricklayer named William Knight was cast for death for being concerned in some house-breaking affairs, but his sentence was mitigated to penal servitude for life. In those days the law was less tender than it is now.

I may mention a third case—that of John Rowe, who entirely in a drunken freak robbed a girl of a bundle of clothes; and while he was undergoing his sentence his father died and left him 2000*l.* It all went to the Crown!

Alexander Mackay, a very promising young fellow but for the drink, who was an apprentice with me in Glasgow, was killed in a prize-fight.

Another man whom I knew, named Thomas Saunders, died from injuries he received in a fight on Primrose-hill. The man who killed him, on being released from the twelve months' imprisonment which he suffered, was so overcome by shame and remorse that he committed suicide by cutting his throat.

The foregoing are a few of the drink tragedies the actors in which I have myself personally known, and in several of the cases I have seen the sad end brought about.

CHARLES NORTH.

Charles North was ruined by a legacy. Paradoxical as this may seem, it is nothing but the simple fact. The legacy was somewhere between 170*l.* and 180*l.* He was a teetotaler for two years or more, and had risen, like all the others who had kept the pledge for any length of time, into a position of comfort and respectability. He was a good singer, and, of course, had formerly been a welcome pot-house companion. I gave him a job (as I did many others) when he signed the pledge, and found him a real warm-hearted fellow. Unhappily, when he got this money, he broke his pledge, and did nothing for nearly twelve months. During this time he was drinking and singing about public-houses. When every farthing had gone he came to me like the Prodigal, and I gave him some pecuniary help. He begged me to give him a job, and I did so. I said,—

"Call upon me to-morrow morning, and we will go over to the work together." I gave him half-a-crown and a shilling, to help him to get his tools. He came the next morning to the house where I used to live. He had some things in his hand, and I had some in mine. We were not seven minutes' walk from the house, when, passing up Vauxhall-road, he suddenly laid his hand upon my arm, gave a short, sharp scream, and fell dead at my feet. I had him taken at once to the doctor, the very man to whom I had taken Jeremiah Kelly.

"Why," said the doctor, "it's not long ago since you brought Jeremiah Kelly here."

"You are right, doctor. It is a melancholy fact that you state, though I fear drink has been at the bottom of it again. He has been drinking for the last eight or ten months. He had a little money left him."

In less than twenty minutes from the time of his leaving my house with me, apparently alive and well, I saw him put into a shell and taken to the workhouse.

THE CASE OF MRS. DAVIS.

I was on one occasion sent to work at Lord Paget's house by Mr. Nettleton, who very often used to employ me before I commenced business on my own account. My son was with me, and we were engaged in fixing some ranges. They offered drink as usual, but I said that we were teetotalers, and that I wished the other men who were with me at the job would not take it. I never would have men about me who would drink during their work-hours if I could help it. When, in reply to another invitation by one of the cooks to have a glass of ale, I said, "No, thank you, I am a teetotaler," the housekeeper, a Mrs. Davis, said, "A teetotaler—you a teetotaler!"

"Yes, I am a teetotaler."

"I wish," said she, "all the world were teetotalers."

"They very soon would be if they took my advice."

By-and-by, in came another cook. She offered me something different to the last.

"Will you have a preserved pear?"

I immediately said, "Yes, thank you," and so I had one.

We got the job finished, and I said to one of the man-servants,—

"Will you allow my son to bring some one who printed a lot of handbills recommending 'Dr. McCurrey's mixture' (teetotalism), and 'Dr. McCurrey's medicine' (the total abstinence pledge)?"

The man-servant, therefore, got this diploma from these bills and called on me. My wife said there was no person of that name—a doctor—living there.

"Yes, there is," he said. "He speaks at the meetings, and I think this is the place."

"What is it you want, sir?"

"Are you Dr. McCurrey's wife?"

"I am James McCurrey's wife."

"Well, I am Lord Paget's servant, and I wish to see Dr. McCurrey. My wife has resolved to spend a sovereign of our own, and that will buy tracts."

We went on very comfortably with this man-servant, who attended the meetings very regularly. We got so well acquainted with him at last that I ventured to ask him a question.

"Where is your good lady?"

"She is not a good lady."

"I wish she was. She certainly ought to be."

He appeared not very anxious to say anything more, and so the subject dropped. It must have been fully two years after this took place that a knock came to my door. It was this very man, and he inquired for "Dr. McCurrey." I should state here that this was a nickname given to me in our *Temperance Intelligencer*—for that was the title of the paper with which we sought to convince the sceptical in those days. He said,—

"I want your tracts."

The result was that he came to the meeting held in the "Original Hall," Chelsea. He said,—

"I should like to hear you speak."

"So you shall, and you shall have it all for nothing."

He came to the very next meeting at which I spoke and signed the pledge, and gave us half a sovereign, which at that time we regarded in the light of what the papers would call "a munificent donation." I said to the Secretary,—

"He is another half-and-half, and I want to see him and his wife join. She is ruining him and killing herself."

He was invited to my house. I saw him at once, and in my rough clothes, so that he hardly knew me. He repeated his tale to me, and away we went to Denbigh-street, Belgrave-square. He went to the door of the house where his wife lived. She had left Lord Paget's service, and he now had a very good situation in Somerset House. He was a teetotaler, but, alas! she was not, as I very soon found out. He said,—

"When I came to the meeting I saw your name—'Dr. McCurrey'—and I thought I would ask for you as that."

"I am not a doctor," I said. "What is the matter with your wife?"

"She has been drinking for a week, and I don't know what to do."

We knocked at the door, and a page-boy opened it. The man took me into the parlour, and I saw that his wife was lying on the sofa. He said,—

"There she is! You see the state she is in."

"Mercy on me!" I exclaimed, as I beheld the pitiable sight. "Are you not ashamed of yourself to be lying there in that position with such a nice family and house?"

She gave a kind of scream.

"Let us have none of that," I said sharply. "You ought to be ashamed of yourself."

I sat down and talked to her, but I was quite in a maze. I felt anything but at home; but God has always made a way for my escape out of such difficulties. What did I think of then? When I was young I used stills for whisky, and it does not require a man to drink much of that liquor to make himself drunk. Of course, like other so-called "jolly fellows," I used to take my drop. The consequence was incipient *delirium tremens*. One night I woke up and cried out,—

"What are all these things coming here for?"

My mother said, "He has got a spell."

The belief in "spells" in those days was very common, and my wife very readily joined in this opinion. They got me a jugful of warm water with a good lot of salt in it. My mother said,—

"I will soon make him better with this."

They gave me nine tablespoonfuls, and this was the way they administered it:—Three tablespoonfuls in the name of the Lord, and three tablespoonfuls again in the name of the Lord, and a third time three tablespoonfuls in the name of the Lord. My poor mother begged of me to take it, and at last I did. I became very sick, and got up and vomited; I then became better. It was no doubt the water and salt that knocked the whisky out of me, and the doctor told me so afterwards. This woman had been drunk for a week. I said,—

"Have you got any fruit in the house—strawberries?"

"I want some ale!" cried the wretched heap on the sofa.

"You shan't have it!"

No strawberries were forthcoming, so I asked for salt and water. It was brought, but the next difficulty was to get her to take it.

"I will guarantee that I will make you all right in less than one hour and a half. I only want you to take a little salt and water."

After a good deal of trouble I got her to take it, and it acted as an emetic. She soon got all right, signed the pledge before I left the house, and went on very well indeed for eight, nine, or ten years. She belonged to a Christian Church, and on one occasion went to hear Mr. Gough. Her husband after a time died, and that was the second great misfortune of her life—the first being her commencing to tamper with the intoxicating cup. She was left very well off. He left her money, besides which the house in Denbigh-street was her own, and she used to let lodgings. When the husband was dying he sent for me. He said,—

"I want to speak to you. I am told that my days are numbered. I want to speak to you about my wife. I have no one that I can talk to like you. I was thinking of leaving the money and my house to my daughters and my son—the one who is going to be a pianoforte-maker—thinking that they would take better care of what I leave."

I said, "Your wife is your wife, and she is closer to you than any one else. If you leave your money to your daughters and your son, you don't know what they may do. Show her you have full confidence in her, and leave your property to her. You can put any restraint you like upon her, but if you leave your money as you propose, you may throw her back again into the dissipation from which she was rescued before."

I persuaded him with such arguments as these, and his wife received the property at his death. One of the daughters is married. The pianoforte-maker, who was then living in Liverpool, is now in London. He was about to commence business on his own account, and knew his mother had the house, and he borrowed her money. I think I could have stopped him, but I did not know the conditions of the father's will. It appears that he said to her,—"You can pawn the lease of this house to a master butcher in Warwick-lane. Mortgage it for 200*l.* to him, and I will pay the 10*l.* interest each year." She did this, and he then wanted more money. The young fellow broke his pledge, and never paid the money. The poor old woman, with this heavy mortgage upon the house, went to live with her daughter, but, by all accounts, didn't feel much at home, and she broke her pledge after keeping it for eleven years. I am thankful to say she never again became the drunkard she used to be, and I understand that she died a happy death. The sole cause of this relapse was that unhappy affair with her family.

THE LIFE AND DEATH OF SANDY M'LAUGHLIN, WITH SOME INCIDENTS IN THE CAREER OF A RELATIVE.

Sandy was a very clever fellow, who could speak seven languages, which he had acquired in his travels about the world. He lived in my relation's house, quite like a gentleman. I became acquainted with him through speaking to him at his residence at a dentist's, who was then doing well, but who since that has gone to pieces through drink. The house was in Old Steine, Brighton, and the events I am now about to relate must have happened about 1860. The house was a rendezvous of Scotchmen on their gala days. One night my brother-in-law and Sandy were sitting drinking, and I warned them very seriously against their drinking habits. Sandy sang his wild drinking songs, and was very merry and amusing—but I could not help thinking of the Scripture words, "The laughter of fools is like the crackling of thorns under a pot," a little flashing and noise, and then smut and smoke. Sandy was a sort of ringleader there, and I left with a dread that something would happen; and, sure enough, something dreadful did happen. There was a lady lived near my relative, and she it seemed was amused by Sandy's jokes and songs, and invited him and my brother-in-law to her house, little expecting what would follow. Sandy took up his abode there as a lodger, and gave a carouse to his friends. They all got mad drunk and sallied out, leaving Ebenezer C——, my relation, in the rooms. He became delirious, and opening the door from the sitting-room into the bed-room, pulled all the bed-clothes out, wrapped them round the chair he occupied, and set fire to them. It was a mercy he did not burn the house and all in it. He was rescued from the flames, and given in charge of the police. A telegram was sent to me on the Sunday. Early the next day I went down, and found the miserable fellow in Lewes jail on a charge of arson.

My brother-in-law was brought to trial. He was very well known and respected by all the doctors, for he was a genius in his particular line of business as a dentist, and was naturally a clever fellow. He was brought up before the magistrate at the police-station, and I went there too. The magistrate said, "Oh! Mr. C——, I am very sorry indeed that a man in the position you once held should have thus given way to intemperate habits. I feel it very keenly to see you standing in that position."

Another gentleman spoke up, and said that something ought to be done for him.

Another got up, and said they had done everything possible for him, until they were tired. During this time I also had been trying to rescue him, though I didn't say so. The lady of the house where the fire happened also appeared, but I can't remember what she said. He was bound over to keep the peace for three months, and since then I have been supporting him, as before stated. On one occasion, when his sister and myself went down to see him, he said, "McCurrey, see how badly I am off for clothes."

I said, "The last time your sister gave you some, you made a bad use of them."

I was turning away from him, when she began to cry. I could not bear this, so I said, "Cheer up! I will do it."

We bought him a nice suit to make him look decent, and when they were all on him, we paid something like 4*l*. for them, and I gave him thirty shillings besides. Will it be believed that he actually changed the new clothes for a ragged suit, got the balance in money, and spent it in drink! But for the drink he was as kind-hearted a man as ever lived.

Twelve months after this my wife and myself went down to Brighton, and found that Sandy McLaughlin had fallen into a very good berth. He was porter at the door of the telegraph office, and seemed to be pretty tidily dressed. I spoke to him, and said, "Sandy, I am glad to see you. Take care and behave yourself, and don't take any more drink."

"The drink," he said, "has been my ruin."

I said, "Try and mend it now." I tried to help him, and gave him good advice.

It was about the summer afterwards when my wife and myself were again at Brighton, and there I saw a tall man carrying two pails of salt water. I said to my wife, "Maggie, I declare if that is not Sandy carrying two pails of water!"

"No, not at all," she said.

"But it is," I said rather sharply. I ran before him and looked into his face, and true enough it was this most unfortunate fellow carrying two pails of salt water for the use of the ladies in the grand houses a little beyond where we were. I said, "Oh, Sandy, Sandy, is this you?"

Merciful me! I could not help crying when I thought of what he was, and of what he might have been.

"Is it come to this?"

Sandy raised his hand, and passed it nervously over his face.

"When did you leave the telegraph office?" I asked.

"I don't know when I left."

"And what are you doing now?"

"I am just carrying up these two pails to the Square yonder. I get 3*d*. a pail."

"And is that what you are doing? Do you think the drink does you any harm now?"

Again his hand passed nervously over his face.

"I told you many a time, Sandy, what it would do for you, but you laughed at me then. Will you hear reason now?"

"It is too late."

"It is not too late."

I did what I could for him, but he was quite right when he said it was too late. The drink had fastened its remorseless fangs upon him, and he now lies in a pauper's grave.

MR. L——.

Mr. L—— was a master-builder in Pimlico, and I mention his case for the sake of showing the extraordinary appetite for drink which some men have, and the lengths to which they will go to gratify it. Will it be believed that he caused himself to be kept in his room for seven or eight days, and was there supplied with drink until he died? A fact like this will be received with a smile of incredulity by some, but not by temperance reformers, who, like myself, have had to face the evil in all its forms. Mr. L—— was one of the most terrible drunkards I ever knew. He seemed to live but to drink, and to help on the drinking system. He was a builder of public-houses, and was always drunk. I knew him in one morning to have no fewer than fourteen glasses of brandy. A life like this may, and indeed must be, a short one; but whether it is a merry one, the intelligent reader must decide.

SAD END OF A PROFESSED CHRISTIAN.

Mrs. H—— used to attend at Sloane Terrace Chapel. She was the wife of a well-to-do hackney-coach proprietor. In the dreadful state of mental imbecility to which she had reduced herself by drink I was asked to go and see her. I found the place going to wreck and ruin; but on the mantel-shelf there still was the collecting-box for the Wesleyan Methodists abroad. It was quite covered with dust. There she sat in the relics of her former finery, replying to all I said by the melancholy words, "Too late, too late!"

"It is not too late," I argued. "The accursed drink is the only thing that is against you. Give that up, and you will be all right again."

She said, "I could not live forty-eight hours without it."

It was in vain that I tried to rouse her. The demon drink had marked her for his own, and though Mr. Nettleton and myself sought to counteract his power, we could not. She ultimately died in a miserable condition.

It has been my lot to see many of the most remarkable cases of reclamation, but with some persons, both men and women—the latter particularly—I could do nothing. Oh, then, is not prevention better than cure? Happy the man who becomes, by the grace of God, a reformed drunkard; but thrice happy he who has never touched the drink or felt the fangs of the monster day by day fastening on him with a firmer and yet firmer hold. Parents, a heavy responsibility rests upon you. Neglect it not, as you shall one day have to give an account.

PERSONAL TESTIMONY OF BENJAMIN H———.

"I was born of respectable parents, who were members of a Christian Church, but by the then supposed need of intoxicating drink, and through the evil tendencies thereof, were much reduced, and had to break up their home and separate, through which I myself had to seek a livelihood amidst great privations. It fell to my lot that my first employer resided at a public-house in Cow-cross, which led me early into drinking habits by accompanying him on his drinking career from public-house to public-house over a period of twelve months, when he filled a premature grave through his habits. I then sought for a living, and fell into the hands of a tailor who was what was then called a 'sweater,' who also lived at a public-house in Clare-market; and it was my lot to work all hours, Sundays included, which again led me into the very hottest of hot-beds of vice for two years. I can distinctly remember, although only between fourteen and fifteen years of age, being with my master, and the man at No. 9, Strand, drinking him for a wager, the result of which was that I was senseless for twenty-four hours; and the doctor, who was sent for, stated that it was doubtful whether or not I should recover. Who would not then have thought that a mother standing so many hours over her son would have seen and felt enough to turn her away from drink? The effect of drink on my appetite, while so young, formed so powerful a habit, that for the next five years I was scarcely ever sober, and the evils passed through are too numerous to state here; the body diseased, the mind all but destroyed, I formed a plan of committing suicide from a steamer proceeding to Gravesend.

"Now is the period I desire to return my sincere thanks to

Almighty God that I was led to hear the voice—the warning voice—of one apparently sent for the express purpose of preventing so fearful an end, and that was the voice of James McCurrey, to whom I have to ascribe, morally and socially, my reclamation from the year 1838 to the present, and with him I commenced to labour in the temperance enterprise.

"At that time (1838) the difficulties were numerous and the opposition great to the cause which we were anxious to promulgate, for we were under the necessity of visiting the various neighbourhoods, and drawing out the insiders of the public-houses, and entering these places and distributing tracts, after which we then had to use our instruments, such as a large hand-bell and fire-rattle. The writer of this sketch has this day (27th February, 1873) seen the two old instruments alluded to. These instruments were requisite to be used because they emptied these dens of infamy, which were at that day of such a degraded character that not one quite so bad can be found in 1873. When the victims to intemperance were thus brought out, they were addressed by the said James McCurrey and myself; amongst them we frequently found men who had fallen from their chapels and churches, one of whom I will mention, connected with the Walworth Wesleyan Chapel. Mr. W—— was a regular attendant at prayer-meetings and at class, besides conducting at home regular religious domestic services, but fell into drinking habits, and thus destroyed his happy home. I have met him frequently and showed him his error, and once he was induced to accompany me to an early prayer-meeting with the hope that he would change his habits. The last time I saw him was with his son (a seaman), a fine young man, on his way to his vessel for abroad. His father said to me, 'We are going to have a parting drop;' but I cautioned him to be careful, and called his mind to the fact that he had once been a Wesleyan. These men, by the time they had reached the vessel, were more than three parts intoxicated, and as the son was waving his hat to his father from the paddle-box in that intoxicated state, his father witnessed his death by drowning, and saw his son's body in the dead-house!

"The result of the labours of a few years formed a temperance society, known as the 'Happy Barn,' in the City of Destruction, on the Bowyer Island, surrounded by a black morass of sin, out of which numbers of families flocked around us. The Ethiopian was made white, the lion tamed, and the wretched drunkard reclaimed. This locality was such a dissolute place, inhabited by the lowest class of Irish, that I at one time nearly lost my life, and was saved by an Irishman who dragged me into his house, and thus protected me. This same worthy man called on me a few days afterwards to inquire to what religion I belonged, as he intended to belong to it, as he felt that I was doing what was right. He was sincere, for he accompanied me to a Wesleyan chapel, and ultimately became an active and reliable member. He could not read, but somehow he obtained help in that respect, and subsequently read the Scriptures, preached, and held meetings at this same City of Destruction, to large numbers of Irishmen, and did a vast amount of spiritual and moral good among a class of people who were given up as thoroughly bad by the Roman Catholic clergy. In all these operations and movements my friend Mr. James McCurrey was active and ready to assist by his presence and advice; and such were the organized plans carried out that sixteen cab-loads, besides other vehicles, were filled by persons to receive Captain McCurrey and the "General," (whose history this is), at one of the meetings in the City of Destruction.

"I desire now to mention a part of the work done in Chelsea near my friend Mr. McCurrey's residence at the Woodenbridge; and the work accomplished by our united exertions, resulting from open-air meetings held by us through years of scorn and persecution. Five halls were founded, and as many as 1600 pledges have been taken in one year, registered at Sydney Hall, Chelsea; through the means of torch-light meetings headed by us, bands of music (formed by our own men) nightly parading the streets, and gathering up the people. Sir Richard Mayne having been written to by our opponents with a view to stop us, we were taken before the police authorities, and bound over to discontinue our operations; but feeling that 'God and truth' were on our side, and that needful strength would be supplied, we quietly laboured on.

"In consequence of our large number of members we were induced, for the purpose of keeping and holding them together, to establish a 'Lodge,' each member distinguished by a silver band, and these were to be seen (being 370 strong) with the 'General' at the various places of worship on the Sabbath-day, clothed and in their right mind, humbly partaking of the benefits offered by the religion of Jesus."

THE CASE OF MR. COLEMAN.

Mr. Coleman was a very respectable man; he used to do all my carting. One day he was taken seriously ill. I went to see him, and after some conversation found that he was as dark as night in reference to his eternal welfare. I spoke to him on this subject, but it appeared to be very distasteful to his wife, and even the minister seemed averse to my talking with him. I said to him, "Well, sir, it is your place to do it, but I do not know why I should not if I think proper."

Shortly after Mr. Coleman broke a blood-vessel in his mouth, and the blood began to run very much. His wife was a very unfeeling woman. Instead of applying remedies which I told her she should to stop the running, she gave him drink in spite of all I could do, and to such an extent that I believe the poor fellow really died intoxicated.

THE CASE OF JOE WALLACE.

Joseph Wallace, or Joe Wallace, as we used to call him, worked for Mr. Cubitt, as a journeyman. When I began business for myself, I employed him. He was a good tradesman, and we got on very nicely. I led him to sign the pledge, but only after a good deal of trouble. I also wanted his wife to sign, and sent my wife to persuade her to do so. She however said that she had a complaint for which the doctor said she must have a drop of gin and water!

"Who is the doctor?" I asked; "I will go and see him."

"His name is Dr. Hunt."

I was not long before I waited on him. He made a sort of a lame excuse, and said she had something the matter which required drink, but that she might do as she liked.

"Are you a teetotaler?" he asked.

"Yes, I am."

"You had better mind your own business then."

"That is what I am doing now, and if you were to let that woman alone and give her no more drink, it would be better for her."

With this I then left him. In the meantime things went very well with Joe. He had a watch in his pocket and comfortable clothes; and he was such a clever man that I raised his wages from 30s. to 2l. a week, and he was well worthy of it, for a man who is sober and industrious is worth any money to his employer. One day my son came to me and said, "Father, I am afraid there is something wrong with Joe Wallace;" and one of the labourers added, "Yes, and I am afraid he has broken the pledge."

"How do you know?"

"Oh, there was a great uproar yesterday in King's Head-court, Chelsea."

I immediately started off to King's Head-court, and found the wife sitting like a Marius amongst the ruins of Carthage. All the best things were smashed, and all the pictures were destroyed.

"What is the matter with you?" I asked.

"Joe has nearly killed me. Look at the eye he has given me. Look at the house. Go and get him to sign the pledge," and she wanted to go down on her knees before me.

"Get up," I said; "go somewhere else for that."

I came out of the house with the view of looking after Joe, and found four or five women outside who seemed to glory in all this spoliation.

"There is your fine teetotaler!" said they sneeringly; and one of them added, "You will find Joe down on the steamboats. He is going to and fro from Battersea to London Bridge."

I went to Battersea Bridge, and found that he had been going backwards and forwards. He was in a very despondent state of mind. I, however, got him to Chelsea, and we talked about teetotalism. I gave him a cup of tea, and then he told me all about his misfortune. He said, "Have you seen my wife? What does she look like?"

"You have been hitting her, Joe."

"I wish she was dead. She has ruined me."

"Never mind; all will be well."

"No, I will cut my throat."

"No, no, you will be all right."

I took him down to my home. It appeared from what he said, that he dressed on the Sunday morning, and went to a place of worship. On leaving that he took a walk before dinner, and on his return he found his wife's brother in the house, sitting with her, and they had a quartern of rum and a pot of ale before them. The brother said, "Come and have a drop of ale."

Joe said rather sharply, "I don't want any of your ale."

His wife said, "Bless my heart, if you are a teetotaler, I am not, and my brother is not; you surely won't be such a niggard as to prevent me treating my brother?"

Joe said that that cut him up very much. The brother took up the ale in his hand and said to Joe, "Don't be a fool; drink, man. Lay hold. Ah! you dare not do it."

When Joe heard him say "dare not," he seized the glass in an unlucky moment and drank it. The scene that ensued was thus described by Joe:—

"I swept the chimney-piece clear of its ornaments, and then pitched into my wife. The brother pitched into me, and I gave him a good whacking, which made him glad to get out of the house."

I put Joe all right again, and sent him back to his wife. It was not long after when he fell again, and ultimately he died a drunkard. His wife also became an inveterate drunkard, and I am afraid her children are anything but what they ought to be.

In concluding this sketch, I will add one fact to show how important it is that all who profess Christianity should support and extend temperance principles. A very near relative of the subject of this history was married, and possessed independent means, enabling her to associate in the so-called respectable circles of society.

Through the custom then existing of wine-drinking and pledging healths, she became gradually a drinker—which ultimately, by reason being weakened, led to worse results, until her character became suspected, and her conduct was watched by those who had once visited her, and she was separated from her husband.

While she was in apparent distress of mind she was visited by the writer, and, of course on professing penitence, became a member of a Wesleyan chapel, and afterwards signed the temperance pledge.

At the Wesleyan chapel she became attached to a leader, who was looked upon as a good and sincere man. On one occasion, when she was paying a visit to his wife, he in mistaken kindness induced her to partake of some drink, and so the pledge was broken.

The former influence of alcohol on her brain became manifest, and she soon spent her income faster than she received it. Her home was broken up—and she died a drunkard's death in a most miserable hovel in the lowest slums of the district.

The class-leader who had caused her fall became more and more addicted to drinking, left the Wesleyan Society, and passed his time in a state of semi-intoxication—some said never absolutely drunk, certainly never sober. He influenced a young married man to join him in his cups, and in this case the young man's career to ruin was very swift; he died of brain fever in a very short time, leaving a wife and eight young children destitute. Soon after, this wretched class-leader followed his victims to the grave, dying miserably as to bodily, worldly, and spiritual matters.

CHAPTER VIII.

BRIEF RECORDS OF THE RESCUED.

I HAVE sometimes seen a little pamphlet telling how a penny became a hundred pounds—and heard many variations of the proverb, "Strive and thrive." My advice would be, Give no money or time to the public-house, and keep clear of either private or social drinking customs, and prosperity (with God's blessing) will follow.

During last year I was told by a very prosperous tradesman—a baker in a very large way of business—that some years ago he heard me at the "White Stiles" on the evils of intemperance. He was then very poor, carrying a basket and selling pies about the streets. If he had eightpence profit at the end of the day it was all. He sold in public-houses, and signing the pledge seemed to shut away his only market. But he determined to try teetotalism; and after a tough struggle with poverty gradually overcame drinking, and proudly he kept on his way, married a good wife, who like himself would not drink, "and now (1875)," he said, "I am worth 8000*l*. That's pretty well, when I began on eightpence!"

THE CASE OF MRS. NEWDON.

I was holding a Temperance Meeting in Westbourne-street,

Chelsea, in the year 1839, when I first met Mrs. Newdon. The meeting-place was a curious one; it was an old shop, and it had no floor and no roof. We, however, hired it; and whilst I was addressing the meeting some other teetotal friends were securing the pledges, which, on the particular occasion I am referring to, numbered from fourteen to twenty. One woman came to me when the meeting was just over, and said,—

"Will you let me sign?"

I said, "Yes; by all means. What is your name?"

She said, "My name is Mrs. Newdon."

I took her pledge, and saw no more of her for three weeks or a month. One day, there was a tremendous row at the "White Stiles" meeting with the policemen, who were about to drag me off to the station-house as usual; when this woman laid hold of the policeman who was near me, and pulled him back and said, "You shan't take that gentleman."

"Are you the woman who signed at the meeting about a month ago?" I asked.

"I am," she replied, and went on pleading with the policeman, who yielded to her.

I may here, before I go further, say that on one occasion when I was sent to the station, and was "cautioned" by Superintendent Lowrie, that a mob of 300 people followed me, and a lot of my friends had their watches in readiness to bail me out.

"Where do you live?" I asked of this woman.

"I live in Jews'-row, sir."

I said I was sorry to see her so much put out about me; but she replied, "If they knew what gratitude I feel! For you have saved me."

Subsequently I learnt her history; and after a consultation with my wife, we gave her an empty room at the top of our house for nothing. She accepted the offer, and lived in our house for some five or six months, and got on very nicely.

We got her to go to a place of worship, and she became a very respectable woman. She got her living by selling tapes, needles, and the like. I spoke to my wife about getting a place for her as a nurse. She was quite fit for that, and I talked to a doctor about the matter. The doctor said he would be glad to do all he could for her. He got her two or three cases to attend to of confinements, at each of which she had 10s. a week and her food for a month.

It was some time after this, perhaps some eighteen months, that we had a grand procession from Cremorne to Kennington-park, and back to Cremorne again, where we had tea. In one of the leading vans there sat an old man, who was very peculiar in many respects. We called him the "Captain," because he had been a sergeant-major in the army.

"Mr. McCurrey," he said to me at the close of the day, "we have had a very nice tea-meeting, and a very nice ride."

"Yes," I said, "we have."

"Do you know who that was—that lady with the black silk dress? If you knew who she was you would be surprised."

"What do you mean?"

"Do you know that she is my lawful wife!"

"Then, in the name of all that's wonderful, why don't you live with her?"

"Oh! no, no, no," he exclaimed, almost with terror.

"Take care. You ought to forgive and forget. Whatever she has done, she is still your wife."

"I pray for her, but I cannot live with her. She has not told this to you. I know that it was you who threw the pledge at her, and caught her with teetotal."

"But why don't you see her and live together?"

"No, no, no."

"Then tell me the reason."

"I was in the Lancers. I went through a great part of the Peninsular War along with Sir John Moore. I was at Mexico also. I came home and got married to her. She had a lot of drunken people about her, and her mother liked drink, and I had a good bit of money. I had 35$l.$ or nearly 40$l.$ in the bank, and she and the rest of them got my book, and by some means or another forged my name and got the money out, and left me penniless."

"Why didn't you tell me all this before?"

"I didn't like to tell you."

"Then make it up now."

"No, no, I will not make it up now, but I will do anything I can for her."

Our conversation was here ended, but it was renewed with Mrs. Newdon and myself.

"Mrs. Newdon," I said, "is that your proper name?"

She said, "I know what you are going to say. I suppose the Captain has been breaking it to you."

She raised her apron to her face, and added, "Poor fellow! I did wrong by him."

I afterwards thought she not only took the money, but went wrong in other ways.

I used to go up to Chelsea once a month, both summer and winter, to give them a speech at the hall that we first started. On one of these occasions when I gave them a lecture, I was going home about ten o'clock, and there was a Wesleyan minister of the name of Loxdale with me. We were walking along arm-in-arm talking on different matters, when Mrs. Newdon came up and tapped me on the arm, and said, "I want to speak to you."

I thought she wanted to draw some of the money she had deposited with me. To my indescribable horror, she simply exclaimed, "Lord Jesus, save my soul!" and dropped as one dead.

It gave me such a shock that I did not know where I stood. I caught her in my arms, and took her into Alsop's, the chemist's shop, and put her down there—tore off her cape and bonnet, and opened her dress. In less time than it takes me to relate it two doctors came in and felt under her ear. They said, "We are just too late. Had we come a little sooner, she might have been saved; but as it is, she may linger for a little, but her death is certain."

True enough, she lived that night out, and the next morning died.

The conduct of the Captain was not the least strange part of this melancholy occurrence. I was the one who broke the intelligence to him.

"Ah, Captain, your wife has gone suddenly home to heaven."

"No, no, no!" he cried, in the accents of a man who could not believe what he heard. "Where is she; what is the matter with her?"

"She is dead, Captain, and there will be an inquest upon her this afternoon."

He was at last forced to believe the truth, and the remorse he felt was, or ought to be, a lesson to those who cherish a grudge against any of their fellow-creatures. He would have given all he had in the world if he had made friends with her before she died. Some twelve months, or perhaps more, afterwards, he himself died.

THE LIFE AND DEATH OF WILLIAMS THE COACHMAN.

This man was once employed in her Majesty's stables as a coachman, before which time he lost his place through drink. He used to know me, and when he saw me on horseback in the great procession passing St. Martin's Church, he said, "If it has got a hold o' Jamie McCurrey I know it will do me some good." I gave him a nod in passing, and subsequently went after him, and got him to sign the pledge. He then told me this story. He said that when he was in the country, doing anything that he could get to do, he went one night into the stable, took away two horses, rode upon one and took the other in his hand, and away he went all the way to Park Lane, close to Hyde Park gates. There is a farrier's about there, or at least there used to be, and he said to him, "I have brought up the two mares." He went on raving in such a way that the people got frightened, and very soon he was attacked by *delirium tremens*. He, however, became a teetotaler, and remained faithful to it for fourteen years, and left his wife a nice grocer's shop, well stocked, and money besides. He died with the Christian's hope.

THE CASE OF MRS. CASH.

Mrs. Cash was the supposed wife of a bricklayer, who was one of my old mates. My wife got her to sign the pledge, and the husband said he would follow her example. Thus the matter was apparently settled. I gave him a job, and he went to work with me for two years. The husband and wife during this time did well. He came to live in my house. This was a nuisance, for they quarrelled tremendously. My wife one day asked her, "What is the reason Mr. Cash and yourself quarrel so? You quite alarmed Mr. McCurrey the other night;" and so my wife drew the truth out of her. She learned that they were not married, and that the quarrel was about his making her his wife. Unless he did so she threatened to leave him. In consequence of this I talked to Cash myself, and brought him so far to the point that he said he would marry her. I told my wife about it, and she was very glad to carry out the arrangements. I lent him a pair of trousers, a coat and waistcoat, and my wife lent various articles of clothing to the future Mrs. Cash. They were married by licence at the church at the bottom of Maddox-street, Regent-street, and I gave her away. A dinner followed this event. We had a nice shoulder of mutton and pie with all the etceteras. The poor woman ultimately died of dropsy, no doubt accelerated by her former drinking habits. My wife was with her in her last moments. Amongst other things the dying woman said, "Oh! Mrs. McCurrey, I was brought up well by my poor mother, and I know what is right as well as anybody, and I never would have lived with Bill so long as I did but for the drink."

She prayed that God would have mercy on her. I talked and prayed with her, and my wife's opinion was that she died a true penitent.

MR. GIBBS.

Mr. Gibbs was a man who had been in the army for a very long time, and had spent the greater part of the period he served in India. He was a peculiar fellow taking him altogether. I have often thought since that he was about the worst and the best I have ever had to deal with. When I first became acquainted, the mode he adopted for introducing himself was, to say the least, the reverse of gentlemanly. It was in Jews'-row, Chelsea, where, when I was addressing the people, he began to swear most vehemently, and applied all the epithets to me of which he could think. After I had been speaking about twenty minutes a change came over the spirit of his dream. He became still. The mouth that was full of blasphemy and cursing became dumb, and the brow that was knit with frenzied madness unbent its furrows, and became expressive of thoughtfulness and emotion. At last he spoke, and swore, with a dreadful oath which is ringing in my ears now, that he would never have but one drop of beer in his life.

"Then," said I, "go directly, and come back and sign the pledge."

He went, came back and signed the pledge, and became a most useful and entirely changed man. He was a good writer, and as Secretary of the George-street Society did it great service, for between nine and ten years. He lived comfortably on his pension and died in comfort and respectability, and was sincerely lamented by a numerous circle of teetotal friends.

JOHN PUNCH.

The name of this ardent worker in the cause might be very frequently mentioned in the course of this narrative. It was my good fortune to be the means of his teetotal conversion in the Westminster Great Hall one Sunday night. He was one of the most useful of temperance men. He was subsequently converted to God. He sent for me on the subject of disquieting thoughts he had about his soul's eternal welfare, and it was my blessed privilege to lead him to the feet of Jesus, where alone he could find peace in believing.

THE CASE OF GEORGE SMART, COLLIER, OF WEST BROMWICH.

He came to London about the time I used to hold meetings at the Pump at Westminster. One Sunday morning, when I was speaking there, I observed him fasten his eye upon me with a steadiness that I could not shake off. I spoke very warmly upon the evils of drink and the blessings of abstinence, and when the meeting was over I said to him, "Well, young fellow, where do you come from?"

"I come from West Bromwich."

"Where on earth have you been since?" I asked, as upon a closer inspection I found that he had no shirt, and was literally clothed in rags.

"I am a poor lad, sir. I only wish my father had been a teetotaler."

"Well," I said cheerily, "you are his son, and may do better than he did." I was impressed with his appearance, apart from the ragged habiliments in which he was clothed. "Come along with me, and we will see if this is not a time for you to redeem the past."

We went to a teetotaler's house, and he got himself washed there. I then got him out of my own wardrobe a clean shirt, a good pair of trousers, a coat, hat, shoes, and stockings. I did not like to get him shaved on Sunday, but that was all he now needed to make him look a very presentable fellow. I gave him some food, and was really frightened at the voracious way in which he proceeded to eat it, for I thought he would have choked himself. I said, "You have had enough. Don't eat any more just now."

With a struggle I got him to leave the food. I then took him home to my house, and my wife didn't know but what he was quite respectable. She did not recognize my clothes on him. My daughter, who is now dead, was a little sharper. When she brought in the dinner she recognized my trousers and waistcoat on him, and went and told her mother, who was downstairs. We drew on to the table; the children sang the grace, and we got on very comfortably. In the afternoon we went to Chelsea, in the evening to the meeting at Westminster. Later still I took him home again and gave him his supper, and took a lodging for him. I told him, as I shook hands with him for the night, to be at my house on the following Monday morning not later than ten minutes before six. I was very much pleased to find that he was there by half-past five.

I took him into my premises and employed him. He could not climb a ladder, neither could he go up a scaffold. If he got on one he could not stand upright, but, true to his collier instincts, he could go down without the least difficulty into the very bowels of the earth. He told me then, and not before, that he was a collier, and how he had left that employment on account of a strike. I said, "Go on and do the best you can, and I will give you work that you can do with comfort to yourself and with satisfaction to me."

He worked for me for about three or four months, and he became quite a favourite in our house. I gave him fifteen shillings a week to commence with, and increased his wages as he became more useful. By this time I had found out where his parents were in West Bromwich, and got some one to write to his father; and, in fact, ascertained that the story he had told me was a genuine one. After he had worked for me for about the before-mentioned period I had one day the job of hoisting up a large piece of timber, and I wanted to get him up at the top. We got him up. I said, "Have you fast hold, Coaley?" for this was the nickname we gave him. "Man alive!" I shouted, "hold fast; your safety depends upon it."

In another moment the piece of timber was hauled into its place on the roof of the house. My son exclaimed, "Oh! father, look at Coaley's hands."

The poor fellow had laid hold of the rope with such a grip that both his hands were skinned and bleeding. We had rather a difficult job to get him down. My wife dressed his hands, and Coaley for the next three weeks lived upon the fat of the land in my house. When he got all right he went to work for me once more, and we got on swimmingly. One Saturday night he said, "Master, I want to speak to you."

"Go on, Coaley. What is it?"

"I don't think I suit you."

"That is my business. What do you want me to do?"

"I don't think I do. I can't climb a ladder."

"I don't want you to. The fact is you are getting tired of me."

"No, I am not."

"Then you have heard of a better job?"

"Yes, I have."

"That's right. It's better to speak out the truth. Where is it?"

"One of the men told me there was a job in Tottenham Court-road to carry out coals and greengrocery at eight shillings a week and my food."

"That is a very good job."

"I want a character."

"What am I to say about you?—that I got a grip of you at the Westminster Pump, and that you hadn't a shirt?"

"No, master, I hope you won't say that."

"Have you been to see them and engaged?"

"No, I would not do that before I had seen you."

"That's right. Always tell the truth."

I got my son to write a letter for him in just these words:—
"The within-mentioned George Smart is a native of West Bromwich. Ever since I have known him, which has now been some few months, he has worked for me, and I have found him sober, industrious, and trustworthy."

He got the situation with this character. Going round the squares with his potatoes, he became acquainted with a young girl whose father had left her 250*l*. He married her, and they are both doing well.

ONE OF OUR LEADING GOOD TEMPLARS.

Mr. Thomas Scott, the genial Office-bearer among our friends the Good Templars, once heard me speaking on Bankside. He also heard me at the Westminster Pump, where he became a teetotaler. That is eleven years ago. May God long preserve his valuable life!

MR. ASKEW.

In March last I was accosted by a gentleman of the name of Askew. He was entirely unknown to me, but on conversing with him I was not a little pleased to find that he signed the pledge at one of my meetings in the Temple Hall, Exeter-street, New-road, at the back of Sloane-street. Regular meetings were held there which I frequently addressed, and it was at one of them in the year 1851 that he signed the pledge. Curiously enough, at the very time he accosted me the bills were out and the arrangements made for a resuscitation of temperance work in this district, and subsequently, in conjunction with the Rev. G. M. Murphy and others, I assisted in opening the place. Mr. Askew told me he was unable to attend the opening meeting, but, he added, that whereas when he signed the pledge he had scarcely a coat to his back, he has now several houses. Ever since 1851 he has lived a consistent, abstaining life, and but for this accidental meeting I should never have known the influence which I had exercised over his life.

THE NOBLEMAN'S SERVANT.

The issue of the bills, to which I have elsewhere alluded, led many persons to believe that I was a medical man.* A nobleman, Lord F——, sent his servant down on one occasion to say he wished to see me. (I may remark that Lord F—— himself was a questionable character. In the end he was found dead in a house of ill fame.) I put on my best clothes, and went to his

---

* See *ante*, "Dr. McCurrey," p. 101.

residence in Belgrave-square. When I got there I was ushered into a room where the noble lord was sitting.

"I have sent for you," he said, "on behalf of one of my servants. By-the-bye, I think he is a countryman of yours. He is a Scotchman."

"Yes, my lord."

"He has been with me for fifteen or sixteen years. He saved my life more than once, and he is one of the best of servants, only he is such a drunken scoundrel that I don't know what to do with him. I would do anything in the world for him. What can you do for him?"

"I can do much for him, if he will only follow my advice. His present condition has been brought about by drinking intoxicating liquors. Let him abstain. We must try and persuade him to do so. Where is he?"

"He's locked himself up in the bath-room."

"Then I must see him."

I was conducted to the door of the bath-room, and whether it was that he heard the smart rap I gave that startled him, certain it is that he did for me what he would do for no one else—opened the door. I held out my hand, and we shook hands. He had only part of his clothes on, and the glassy stare of his eyes and the colour of his face showed me that he was suffering from an attack of *delirium tremens*.

"How are you?" he said.

"First-rate, and I wish you were the same."

The servants left us together.

I said, "Your master has been really very kind to you, and I heartily wish you would give up this habit."

I then turned to the noble lord, who was standing near the door, and said, "My lord, you are desirous of doing all you can for your servant, and so you ought, for you say he has been the means of saving your life more than once."

"That is quite true, and I have no fault to find with him but the drink."

"Then the case is clear, if he never takes strong drink he will never become drunk. I want you, my lord, to sign the pledge, and show him an example, and help him thus to keep it. I also want his wife to do the same. She, I understand, is the housekeeper here."

"What did you say?" he inquired, a little perplexed.

"I wish you to sign the pledge to abstain yourself, so that he may have your countenance and support."

"I can't do anything of the kind," he said; "what have I got to pay?"

"Nothing at all. I am not a doctor, but a bricklayer, and my only object in coming here was to rescue this poor man, and by God's help, my lord, I will try and do it."

I have alluded to the sad end of the noble lord himself, but it affords me the liveliest satisfaction to say that the servant joined our society, and became one of our best teetotalers. He also joined the Rev. S. Beardsall's chapel, at Pimlico, and was a useful member there.

The following letter is a record of—

A TEETOTAL FAMILY OF FOUR GENERATIONS.

"I take this opportunity of giving you the particulars you require with great pleasure. I will do the best I can myself. I first signed the pledge at Hammersmith, with my sister, on the 11th day of November, 1840, and have kept it faithfully from that time. My sister kept it faithfully until her death. She died on the 25th December, 1866.

"My father signed the pledge at the Primitive Methodist Chapel, Hammersmith, on the 21st of February, 1842, and kept it faithfully until his death. He had an accident while under the employ of Mr. Tisdall, of Kensington, by falling from a scaffold at Holland Farm, Kensington; was taken to St. George's Hospital, and died on the 1st day of March, 1854. The accident happened on the 21st February, 1854.

"Mr. Tisdall took the affair in hand, and the temperance friends bought the ground, and he was interred at Brompton Cemetery, March 12th, 1854.

"Sir, you know all particulars of that day's proceedings.

"He died at the age of forty-nine years.

"My mother signed the pledge in February, 1845, and kept it faithful until her death. She died on the 9th of November, 1873.

"My brother signed the pledge on the 2nd February, 1843, and has adhered to his principle, and is married to an abstainer, and has five in family, all abstainers for life.

"I myself married a teetotaler in the year 1847. My husband, William Durrant, signed the pledge on the 4th day of January, 1845, under Mr. James McCurrey, at the Temperance Hall, New-road, Sloane-street, Chelsea, and is still an earnest teetotaler. We have twelve children living, life-abstainers, never taking it even medicinally, two daughters and one son married, all teetotalers; seven grandchildren, these being the fourth generation of teetotalers.

"Dear sir, I may have put down more particulars than you require, and there may be some more you require that are not in; if so, you can put on one side anything you do not require, and if you need more, if you send me word, I will reply, if I can answer you, with the greatest pleasure.

"Hoping you are quite well, and thanking you kindly for the interest you are taking in the temperance cause generally, may your valuable life be spared many many years to labour on with us in so glorious a cause! With kind love,

"Yours truly in the cause,

"A. DURRANT."

CHAPTER IX.

THE CASE OF MATTHEWS.—MISCELLANEOUS RECORDS AND NOTES OF EXPERIENCE.

THIS man was a drinking, swearing fellow. He was a cobbler, and earned a good deal of money. I however got him to give up drink, and after a time he became a member of the Wesleyan chapel which I attended in Great Queen-street. He was regular in his attendance at Divine worship. This continued for two years and a half. We were neither of us at this time teetotalers, but were sober men. I was one day sent for to go and see him. At this time, I should say, he belonged to the old Temperance Society, the members of which bound themselves to abstain from spirits. I also belonged to this. When I went I found that one of Matthews's companions, or "mates," was taken very ill with cholera, and Matthews was sent for because it was known that he would pray with and for him. He went, but when he came back he was taken ill himself. This was on a Saturday morning, and it was about eleven o'clock that he was taken ill. When I came home from my work I went to see him, and found him very ill. The doctors were there putting mustard plasters to his feet, rubbing his legs, and so on. I talked to him very seriously about spiritual things. The doctor at last said, "Now, Mr. McCurrey," (for he knew me) "you must withdraw. It is not right for you to be here."

At that time the cholera was raging. It would be about the year 1832. My wife was present, as was also the wife of Matthews, but we were all ordered from the room, for there was no chance of his recovery.

"I want to see Mary and the children," said the poor fellow.

I said, "Let him kiss them;" for I felt for him very much. He shook hands with his wife, but she was rather frightened, and didn't kiss him. He kissed the children, and then turning to me, he said, "McCurrey, you have been a good friend to me. Will you let me hold your hand?"

"Yes," I said, "I will;" and the doctor added, "He may."

I stayed with him till eleven o'clock at night, and he got worse and worse. I talked to him all the time. I asked, "Well, Bill, how do you feel?"

"I feel bad all over, and believe I won't get over it."

"And how do you feel in reference to your eternal salvation?"

"I will tell you what I feel," he said, as the tears rolled down his face. "I feel sorry I did not know the Lord Jesus sooner, and I am sorry I have not served Him more faithfully and better;" and with that he fell back a corpse, still keeping hold of my hand.

Next morning I followed my friend to St. Pancras, in company with two more. Nobody else would go after him. He was in health on Saturday morning, and was buried on Sunday morning.

THE CASE OF MR. DOVE.

Mr. Dove was one of Mr. Cubitt's deputy-foremen over the

labouring men, and was very useful, inasmuch as he knew how to keep them to work. He was in Cubitt's when I was there, and I got him to sign the pledge. At the time of the cholera he lost three nice boys, and he broke the pledge through these misfortunes. He used to say that brandy was a good thing for cholera. I went to see him when the fatal disease struck him, and found him in a dreadful state. I watched him and got him all right again, and to leave off the drink. He, however, went into drinking habits again. On one occasion he fell into the river, and was barely rescued with his life. This served as a warning to him for the remainder of his life, and he lived some ten or twelve years afterwards a consistent member of the National Temperance League. During his illness he told me that his brother was a Wesleyan minister, and that they were the children of pious parents. I was with him in his last moments, and firmly believe he has gone pardoned to a happy home.

JEREMIAH KELLY.

This man worked for me as a teetotaler for a considerable time. The pest of his life was a drunken, dissipated wife. I was at that time just finishing the house in which I lived so long—Upper Dorset-street. That would be about twenty-two years ago. I said to Kelly on one occasion, "Where have you been to all this time?" for he had been absent from his work.

"Oh, that woman, that woman! I wish she was in her grave. I gave her all my money on Saturday, and could not get as much as a cup of coffee from her for my breakfast this morning. She has spent it all."

"But you yourself have been drinking this morning!"

"Yes, I have. I am lost."

"Nonsense, you must reform; but mind what you are up to going up that ladder."

He was carrying up chimney-pots. I saw his unsteady gait, and said, " You mustn't go up any more."

" Why won't I go up? faith, I will."

" Faith, you won't."

" Why not?"

" Because I say you won't."

" I am as able to go up as any man you have got."

I, however, insisted. I can scarcely say why I was so positive, but there was something in his face after the disturbance with his wife that made me firm. I ordered him away into the foundation of the next house; told him to take a shovel and work there. He took up the shovel—gave a scream, and dropped dead at my feet. This was terrible. Here was the fourth person who, within a comparatively short time, had fallen at my feet dead—Charles North, Mrs. Newdon, Izard, and now Jeremiah Kelly. I trembled like a leaf shaken by the breeze.

MRS. POWELL.

She was a steadfast member of the Wesleyan body for about forty years, and as soon as she heard of teetotalism she signed the pledge. She said, " My son is in the army, and I will do it to set him an example, and for no other reason." Mrs. Powell's husband was mate in a large ship which was in the China trade, but he was lost by drink. Mrs. Powell wrote to the regiment in which her son was, but he sent home word to say that he had been a pledged abstainer in the army, and was coming home to see her. He was soon stationed at Hampton Court, and she went to see him. When poverty came over her, I used to help her a little. There were a great many people who belonged to us, and who got their living by selling fish and vegetables and the like. Mrs. Powell, when her husband died, used to sell crockery-ware out of a basket. When I used to see her I used almost always to ask her how she was getting on, and perhaps say, "Here's a shilling to get a cup of tea." She would respond by saying, "Here is a jug to carry home to Mrs. McCurrey," but, of course, I would not take the poor woman's jug without paying her. One day I was returning from the Westminster Bank, where I had been cashing a cheque, when I saw two dogs fighting. The result was that they upset the poor woman's basket, and broke her dishes. When she recovered from the state of confusion into which this had thrown her, she cried, "Oh! Mr. McCurrey, the devil set the dogs on me."

She died a Christian and a teetotaler, and her son is, doubtless, an abstainer to this day.

AN ECCENTRIC CASE OF AN OLD LADY AT LEWES.

This was an old lady, decidedly one of the most curious of her sex whom I had ever met. She praised God, but stoutly declared she would not sign the pledge. I had to speak in the town, and this old lady was present. The people told me I would find her a terrible Tartar. As I went on with my address she repeatedly gave vent to such exclamations as "Bless the Lord!" "Bless His Holy Name for ever!" "Glory, glory, glory!" I looked over at her and said, "What is the matter with you? We don't want two to speak at one time."

However she went on, and I really began to think I should have to stop, as all the rest who had preceded me had been obliged to do.

"Is this lady a teetotaler?" I asked.

"No, sir."

I tapped her on the shoulder, and said, "I wish to speak to you, if you please. Are you a teetotaler?"

"No."

"Won't you be one?"

"I don't need to be."

I lifted up my hands and said, "O Lord God Almighty, look down upon this poor old lady, for she says she wouldn't give up her beer if all the people were drunkards, and if they all went to perdition."

The old lady trembling said, "I will sign the pledge."

"Sooner than an old lady should die blind," I exclaimed, "I would leave no means untried of opening her eyes."

I can truly say that this old woman's adhesion was at that time thought to be a great prize, and certainly she became a very industrious woman in the cause.

THE PUBLIC-HOUSE LICENCE.

As I have before intimated, I would not show any of my houses on the Sunday, although many people seemed to prosper very much by doing so. At one particular place the difficulty I encountered in selling the houses was very great in consequence of the nuisance caused by a public-house. I may here remark that our friends of the United Kingdom Alliance do well to remind the people of the depreciation to which their property is subjected by the proximity of public-houses. Well, this public-house got a licence for singing, and the very rakings of the pit used to assemble for carousal. My houses being empty, the scum of the earth, who used to frequent this tavern, were in the habit of going through my houses, and they were not slow at committing all kinds of destruction. So much was this the case that I spoke to Mr. Cubitt about it. He offered to help me if I liked to take action. So I got an old coat and hat, with boots and trousers to match, and watched the public-house. On two or three occasions, in the course of my vigils, I saw a fight going on inside, and a woman tumbled out of doors. I gave the publican warning that I would complain to the magistrates, but practically the answer I received from him was that he was going to make application for a music-hall licence. I collected subscriptions amongst the respectable inhabitants, and Mr. Cubitt gave me a solicitor free of cost. I got up a very strong petition, and, armed with this, I hailed for the Clerkenwell Sessions House to oppose the licence, and at the time there were applications for two or three similar licences. There was a man named Sam Collins, a comic singer, who at the same time applied for a licence for a house at Hendon, or near it, I forget which; but the clergyman of the place opposed, and bore testimony to the evil the place did to his Sunday-school boys and girls, and the magistrates, instead of allowing him to have another licence, stopped the one he already had. Sam Collins was originally a plasterer in Westminster, but left that for the " comic " line. He died a few years ago, leaving a sort of public-house concert-room in Islington, which still goes by his name.

The publican, who wanted the licence for the neighbourhood in which my houses were situated, also came fortified with a petition numerously signed. When he presented it, I, knowing the way it was got up and by whom it was signed, got—well, perhaps, a little excited, and wanted to speak, but the usher of the court called me to " order." My lawyer told me it was no use opposing it, and that was about the sum and substance of the help I got from *him*.

" Gentlemen," I said, appealing to the magistrates in spite of the calls to order, " I may be wrong in addressing you, but the publican knows very well that what he has put on paper before you is untrue, and that his house is a disgrace and pest to the neighbourhood."

Just at that moment, as God would have it, my eye caught sight of two of the policemen who were with me the night the woman was thrown out at the door.

"Were not you there," I said, appealing to them, "and saw that woman thrown out of this man's tavern?"

"Put the gentleman in the box," said the presiding magistrate.

In the box I was accordingly placed and sworn.

"Have patience," said the magistrate; "take it gently;" and no doubt I had need of the caution, for I was labouring under terrible excitement. I mentioned what I had seen.

Mr. Ribton, the lawyer, engaged on the other side, said,—"You said that my client had not a respectable signature to his petition."

"I did."

"Do you happen to know Dr. P——?"

"I do."

"Is not he a gentleman?"

"If he is, he is not acting like one, seeing that he has no business to sign the petition."

"Why not, pray?"

"Because he is only a lodger, and I have got the signature of the man to whom I sold the house, and who is consequently the proprietor."

Mr. Ribton sat down.

This Dr. P—— was a Wesleyan Methodist and a class-leader, but the secret of the signature business was that he waited on the publican's family when they were ill.

"Gentlemen," I said to the magistrates, "I have got over 15,000*l.* or 16,000*l.* invested in house property in this neighbourhood, and it is not mine. My property is already mortgaged, and if this is to go on it will be destroyed. These houses are not dog-kennels, but have ten rooms each, fit for the habitations of even such gentlemen as sit upon this bench, and they let at 70*l.* a year.

At last they stopped the licence, and I got 5*l.* for my

expenses. Had this matter been in the hands of the respectable ratepayers they would have made much shorter work of it.

THE OPPOSING MINISTER.

In the early days of the temperance reformation it need hardly be said that things did not go so smoothly as they do now. We not only had ministers of the Gospel preaching, but even praying against us. They also made themselves very active in turning us out of our meeting-places, and particularly those schools over which they had jurisdiction. I have many a time stood in Jews' row, Chelsea, with a minister or local preacher, Bible in hand, warning the people not to listen to me. They said I was one of those men who were to come in this latter day, to try to establish the principles of sobriety as a redemption for the soul of man. I replied to one of these individuals on one occasion, and, perhaps, on more than one, "My good fellow, if you know no more of Christ than that, you have no right to stand up as a teacher. You yourself want to be taught. No man who understands salvation would ever say that anything but the work of Christ can secure the immortal soul for time and for eternity. If we would be saved we must turn to Jesus, and with His love in our hearts God will give us peace."

Those about me could thus hear and judge of the truth of the assertions which my opponent was making. In those early times the temperance men were to a large extent rescued drunkards, and were ignorant, by reason of the debasement which had hitherto surrounded them, of even the first principles of Christianity; but the great message of God to a lost world was so often proclaimed that their hazy notions of the work of redemption soon dispersed, and upon many a soul there dawned the sweet star of peace and of faith in a Redeemer's love. The charge against us made by many of these ministers (who, I am bound to believe, made them in all sincerity) was, that by teetotalism we were trying to lessen the great gift of God, and that we were putting up something in its place, and thus misleading ignorant men. This minister even carried his opposition so far that he distributed bills announcing that he was going to deliver a lecture on "The evils of total abstinence, and the blessings of true temperance." I repeat here that there could be no doubt but that in what he was doing he thought he was serving the great end of his mission. I immediately on seeing one of these bills made up my mind to go. I did so, and several of my temperance friends were with me. He opened his meeting with the singing of a hymn, in which the crowded audience heartily joined, including myself and friends. He then offered prayer, in the course of which he prayed—I mention this with the greatest reluctance, but it is necessary to the completeness of the narrative—that Christian people might be saved from this "water-butt righteousness," and that God would hasten the day when all the water would be turned into wine. He repeated, "O Lord! hasten that happy day when all the water shall be turned into wine, that the glory of Christ may be seen."

I rose up, and, in the excitement of the moment, said, "O Lord! answer not the prayer of this man, for if all the water is turned into wine what shall become of the people, what shall become of the cabbages, what shall become of the fish?"

He closed his prayer and commenced his lecture, and in the course of it he said very many things which it was hard for me to bear. Amongst others, "My brethren in the Lord, be careful and watchful, because these poor deluded teetotalers are like the Roman Catholics. They are grasping at the shadow instead of the substance."

"I beg you, sir," said I, "to let the Roman Catholics alone.

If you are a minister of Christ, let the people see it by your actions as well as by your words."

He still proceeded, or rather tried to, but he could not get on at all. As he continued, there was an Irishman of the name of Kelly who had become a teetotaler, and who on hearing his religion aspersed became very excited: " Let the poor Roman Catholics alone, and mind your own business. If they were no better than you are, you would have been in ——" (mentioning a certain place).

I had made some stir by my interruptions, but this caused a still greater one. A policeman was sent for, and three persons and myself were given in charge. On this occasion I adopted the plan which proved so successful with Mr. Alsop. I gave the minister in charge for meddling with things he had nothing to do with. The result was just the same. The minister refused to come down, and I declined to go until he did. The sequel is a sad one. In about six or eight months he fell through drink. He lost his pulpit and his chapel, and both became permanently empty.

Mr. G. C. Campbell at that time had commenced his useful work, and aided the society greatly in what followed. I proposed that we should buy the place, and promised 10*l*. towards it. My wife said she would be 5*l*. towards it, and a milkman, who was a good friend of ours, then said that he would give the same. We clubbed together, and Mr. Campbell, who was treasurer of the Rechabites, said we could borrow the rest out of the Rechabites' Society; and so we borrowed the rest of the money, and bought the chapel. We have had it now for more than thirty years; it is Sydney Hall. We took all the chapel furniture out, &c., turned the place pretty nearly upside down, and made it a fine temperance hall. When my son died some time ago he left this Society 600*l*.; 100*l*. at the present time, and 500*l*.

when his wife dies. The 100*l.* was used for the renovation and refurnishing of the hall, and Mr. Campbell and myself have been holding meetings there lately. The assistance this hall was to us in rallying our members, and in confirming them in the teetotal faith, is more easily imagined than described.

"THE MAN WHO INVENTED GAS."

Many of the readers of this will remember that Mr. Campbell has frequently told an amusing story which happened in the Great Hall, Westminster. One Sunday evening I was directing the people to look to God as their Saviour, and was speaking of a dying man whom I had just visited, and who sent for the minister of the Gospel, when a man in the meeting rose up, and said, "The man who invented gas has done more than all the parsons, and priests, and popes in the world."

When Mr. Campbell rose, he very wittily turned the laugh on the fellow by saying, "When our chairman, Mr. McCurrey, is dying, he will send for the minister; but when you are dying, you can send for the gas-fitter."

My friend, Mr. Balfour, on hearing this amusing reply, said it would be well to add to the record that WINSER, the ingenious man who introduced gas into London, and after many difficulties and impediments thrown in his way succeeded in lighting Pall Mall, was not himself benefited by his skill. He, like many of the cleverest workmen, was overcome by his appetite for drink. In proportion to his gains were his temptations. He fell into debt, and all the misery of pecuniary embarrassment, went abroad, and died in great distress in Paris. Mr. Balfour in 1858 was in Paris, and saw Winser's monument in the cemetery of Père la Chaise, with the inscription "EX FUMEN LUX"[1] on the tomb. After the

---

[1] Out of smoke, light.

record of his name and the mention of his invention, it is insinuated that his own country, England, was ungrateful to him—an unjust charge. It is impossible to help a man who will not help himself. Poor man! like many of the best and wisest among scientific and literary men he loved the drink, and so fell a victim to alcohol.

THE CASE OF IZARD.

Izard was a master carman, but he did not attain to this position until he had signed the pledge. He had three brothers. His own Christian name was Shadrach, and those of two of his brothers were curiously enough, Meshach and Abednego. Before becoming a teetotaler, Shadrach Izard was a brickmaker in Mr. Thomas Cubitt's employment. When he became a teetotaler he very soon was able to employ some men to work under him in the field, where he made bricks at so much per thousand. He signed the pledge in the George-street (Chelsea) Hall, after an address which I delivered. He prospered very well, and managed to buy two or three horses. By-and-by we began to miss him from the hall, and when this was the case I always made it a point to go after him, or send my wife, or another of the teetotal friends. They went after him, but did not succeed in finding him. One day I was walking in the street, when I saw Izard. He tried to avoid me, but it was of no use.

"How are you getting on, Izard?"

He said, "Very well."

"I haven't seen you at the meetings lately: are you still a teetotaler?"

"No; I am not."

"How is that?"

"Well," he said, "a man like me who has got to do with builders--unless I have a glass of ale or a drop of gin with them now and then, I do not know how I could get on. I have got plenty to do."

"Take care," I said. "Teetotalism brought you from an awful state of drunkenness and poverty; it made you a foreman in the brick-field, got you horses and carts, and it will make an example of you yet. You are an ungrateful fellow."

He went away. I sought him out again, but could not find him. One day, as I was walking along the street, my son said, "Come here, father; there is Mr. Izard, the carman, half naked. I am sure he is mad. He is going up and down the road talking to everybody." And, true enough, when I approached there he was. He had broken out of his wife's grasp when he was in bed, under the influence of *delirium tremens*. I got hold of him, and asked, "What is the matter?"

He came up to me and clapped me on the shoulder. I said, "Come along home;" and after much difficulty I got him there. In the course of the journey I said to the wife, "Mrs. Izard, if you don't look after your husband this will be the saddest day's work that was ever done, so far as you are concerned. Why don't you keep him in-doors?"

She replied, "The doctor has been here, and has ordered him two glasses of gin every three hours."

I am afraid I gave utterance to a very rude expression towards the doctor, but I added, "He will kill him. Who is the doctor?"

She would not tell me. By this time, as before stated, we had got him home and put to bed; and, thinking he was all right, I left the house. I was not gone ten minutes or a quarter of an hour when some one ran to me, and exclaimed, "Mr. McCurrey, Izard is down amongst the boats, and I am afraid he will get killed!"

I ran to the spot indicated, and found him with nothing but

his trousers and shirt on. The men about him were very much frightened, but he became tolerably quiet when he saw me. He said, "You are a good fellow, 'Currey."

I got him away from the spot, but not without some struggling on his part. I gave him two or three shakes, and then saw him home. I told the wife to be sure and keep him in the house, and to give him some arrowroot. I said I would go and see the doctor, but she would not give me his name; and I am sorry to add that it was through her that Izard broke the pledge. I then left, but not until I had made her promise that she would look after him well. Oh, dear! oh, dear! I had not been gone half an hour when up he got, and obtained more gin for himself. He ran out of the house. He was brought back and tied down to his bed. There he lay kicking and swearing, with the froth flying out of his mouth. It was in this condition that he passed into eternity. He had been a teetotaler four years when he broke the pledge.

THE CASE OF IZARD'S WIFE.

To this sad story must be added one equally sad. It shows the retribution which often in this world overtakes those who have been doing wrong. When Izard died he left a good deal of property; at least, a good deal for a man in his position. His wife, who inherited it, was never a teetotaler. When Izard died she became acquainted with another man. Her property was speedily sold, and with the proceeds the man opened a "Jerry shop." He died, and she went to the workhouse. To say that everybody was glad was only to say the truth, for her inconsistency was great, and her influence over her husband was only for evil.

EXETER HALL.

I remember well a temperance meeting held in this building at which Daniel O'Connell and a famous bishop were the principal speakers. I am afraid that on that occasion I fell finally and irrevocably out of the good graces of the bishop. The bishop made some gratuitous remarks about religion, and said if he saw the Pope coming in at one door he would walk out at the opposite one. The Right Rev. Father was not a teetotaler, and knew very little about the subject, seeing that he wanted to prove that sugar might generate into alcohol in the stomach to such an extent as to cause the poisoning of a woman. He referred to the case of Stowell, who was executed for poisoning a woman by giving her some peculiar kind of fruit. I was called upon after the bishop, and said that if he were one of the "pillars" of the Church she would very soon crumble to pieces. There was a roar of laughter at this. Daniel O'Connell shook me by the hand, and called me a true countryman, evidently taking me for an Irishman.

"I am not an Irishman," I explained.

"You are a true man, and God bless you!"

I think this meeting was convened by the old London Temperance League.

ST. KATHERINE'S DOCKS.

At the opening of this place, in 18—, there was a scene which I hope never to see again. Ham and beef were in abundance, but drink, drink, drink was in still greater abundance. When English and Irish navigators are drunk they invariably fall out, and the scene which occurred on this occasion would have disgraced the most barbaric region which the zealous missionary or the travel-stained explorer has ever yet discovered.

TEMPERANCE MEETING IN EXETER HALL.

CHAPTER X.

MISSIONARY WORK IN DIFFERENT PLACES.

I REGRET that I have not kept anything worth calling a journal of my visits to different towns in the provinces, seaside places, &c. I jotted down anything which struck me at the time; but I fear, nay, I know, I left out as much that was interesting as ever I remembered. Suffice it that I tried to obey the injunction to "sow beside all waters." Go where I would I found intemperance, and therefore had work to do, and did it to the best of my ability, in faith and prayer looking for a blessing and not labouring in vain.

MY WORK AT DOVER.

I went to Dover to advocate the temperance cause shortly after the year 1840, and held several meetings. I used to go down two or three times in the course of the summer. I held some of the meetings in the open air, and some of them in the schools and other places of that kind. I also held meetings in the large room of the "Black Horse Tavern." One morning I saw one of the 92nd Highlanders lying, with his kilt, hose, and feathers, in the harbour, smothered in the mud. He had fallen in while drunk the night before. I immediately addressed the people, who were looking on at this most mournful sight, and said, "Here is some of strong drink's handiwork. I daresay the man who now lies before you was one not habitually given to intoxication, but here he lies an awful warning to those who tamper with the destroyer. Be warned by me, my good friends, and forswear drink from this moment for ever."

When I was at the Charing Cross Railway Station, ten or twelve years after this, a man wearing the official uniform of the South Eastern Railway came up to me and asked if I were still a teetotaler.

I said, "Yes."

He said, "I signed the pledge many years ago at one of your meetings at Dover."

"Then you were not then what you are now," said I.

"Nor I never should have been if it hadn't been for teetotalism. Don't you remember, when you used to come down to Dover, you always came down third-class, and they used to leave you at a certain station below Ramsgate, and kept you waiting till the next train?"

"Yes, I remember all that."

"And you used to sit down there with the signalman?"

"Yes."

"Well, that's me. After that I was put on to be a guard, and then I was advanced still further, and now I am here, and a teetotaler."

SEASIDE MEETINGS.

Amongst the places on the South Coast where I have held meetings I may include the Black Rock and the Level at Brighton, Hove, Portsmouth, Carisbrook, and Ventnor. These were all convened at my own expense.

THE CASE OF SALE, WHO WAS EXECUTED FOR THE MURDER OF BELLCHAMBERS.

Sale was a man who always dressed himself like a sailor.

He became a member of our teetotal society, and got on for a time very well. He was a pedlar to all appearances, but if any one was asked how he got his living I very much question if he could have given a very decided answer. He was very fond of dancing, and our hall was made use of for the purpose. At first the more timid-minded amongst us tolerated this, but we found that dancing was becoming of more importance to some of the people about us than anything else. It became, therefore, absolutely necessary that the dancing should be stopped, and stopped it accordingly was, though in as kind a way as possible. Sale became extremely annoyed at this. He left us, and, poor fellow! in an evil hour he broke his pledge.

Mr. Bellchambers was also a man who had broken his pledge. He was, however, in a responsible situation, being no other than the manager of the Chartered Gas Works. One day he had been drinking heavily, as usual, and was watched by Sale and some of his companions going down King's Head Court, where a brutal attack took place—a row in which Sale smashed his head. Bellchambers died, and Sale was executed for the murder. When speaking in the open air I used to allude to the cases of these two men as an awful instance of the results of breaking the pledge. I went to see Sale's unfortunate children, and did what I could to keep the roof over their head. Sale was a man who bid fair to do well, but, alas for him! knowing the right, he yet pursued the wrong.

STORMY MEETING AT DARTFORD.

In about the year 1840 (three years after I had signed the pledge) I was invited to commence the temperance work in Dartford. Mr. Collins, of Walworth, very kindly accompanied me. The letter of invitation came from a young man who had interested himself in the cause, and we walked it on foot. The roads were not in the best state, and to add to our difficulties it began to rain. It took us five hours to walk it, and a very unpleasant journey it was. We started about ten o'clock in the morning, and didn't get there till three or four in the afternoon. When we got into the town, the next point was to find our correspondent. He was a journeyman shoemaker. In course of conversation we talked of who should be asked to take the chair.

The young man said, "There is a very nice gentleman, a minister of the Church of England. Can we get him to take the chair? I think we can."

"Where can we get a meeting-place?" I next asked.

"There is the Town Hall," was the reply, "which you can get for ten shillings, lights and all."

We paid that between us, and thought ourselves fortunate in getting so good a place at so cheap a rate. We then gave the bellman eighteen-pence to go round the town and "cry" the meeting. Having fairly started the bellman, we went to look at the arrangements in the Town Hall, and perceived that it was lighted with candles. Imagining that everything was now going on smoothly for a successful meeting, we went and regaled ourselves with a cup of coffee and a roll and butter each. Our meal was interrupted by hearing that the bellman could not call the meeting. The fellow was so drunk that he could scarcely stand, so I went round with him. He had no occasion to show me the way about the town; I knew it well, for I had passed once through it as a tramping bricklayer, and had slept in the Court-house. The result of our exertions was a Town Hall literally packed. The idea of teetotalism was thoroughly new, for this was absolutely the first teetotal meeting that had been held in it. [I went down shortly before these lines were written, and the place would hardly hold the people. Two men recognized me, both of whom became teetotalers at the first visit, and both of whom have remained so ever since.] The audience, I found, was chiefly composed of the hands employed in the powder and paper-mills, and most of them wore white hats. The clergyman, who had in the interval agreed to take the chair, came according to promise. He was received with many good-humoured but somewhat annoying remarks. I was very thankful to see him, as it was something like a guarantee for good order. He sat down, and I gave out the hymn, "Rise and shine." We all sang together, and the effect was *not* harmonious. When we had done, the chairman rose, and spoke to the following effect :—

"I don't know these men. They came to my house and asked me to preside over this meeting. I believe it has something to do with the temperance society. I am not a temperance man, and don't suppose I ever will be. I believe that all hard-working men ought to have a pint or two of good home-brewed beer to enable them to do their labour. (Cheers from the meeting.) Drunkenness is no doubt wrong, but still I am in favour of beer for working men."

It was then my turn to speak. I reminded the chairman that I had invited him to preside, and not to cut the ground from under my feet. I had not come there for their money, or for anything else save their moral and material good. I had come there as one who being once made miserable by the drink had now been made happy by teetotalism.

During this harangue the chairman was continually interrupting me, until at last, losing all patience, I told him to leave the chair altogether. He took up his hat and walked out. When he had gone the turmoil was something terrible to behold. I got up again to speak to them. (They had previously put poor Mr. Collins down.) The platform was crowded with seemingly respectable persons. A minister belonging to the Baptist denomination very kindly came into the chair, and spoke to the meeting. They listened to him most attentively. I then rose again, but a man, respectably dressed, began calling out, "It's a lie! it's a lie!" I said, "Who are you?" One of the fellows in the meeting said, "Why that's the nephew of the brewer."

"Then will you let that man upset this meeting, and prevent my speaking?"

"No! no! no!" cried the people, and, suiting the action to the word, they seized him by the neck, and conveyed him rather roughly down the steps of the Town Hall.

"Go on, bricklayer."

I did go on. I sang them a song with a rattling good chorus. One of the forms gave way during this song, and a number of people fell down, but mercifully there was no one injured. I never felt more under the influence of deep emotion than I did at that meeting. At the conclusion of my speech twelve signed the pledge, and amongst them were three of the biggest drunkards in Dartford.

One or two of them very kindly inquired if I and my companion were going home that night. I told them we were, and that I was only a journeyman. We had a cup of coffee with some of these friends, and then they declared their intention of seeing us out of the town. We left Dartford at about half-past eleven at night, and walked all the way to London. My friend, Collins, went to Walworth, and I went to Chelsea. When we were going over Shooter's Hill, there were two men and a woman who made up to us.

One of them said, "Good morning."

"Good morning," I said.

"Going to London?"

"Yes."

"What's o'clock?"

"I don't know."

"Haven't you got your watch?"

"Yes, and I intend to keep it."

Poor Mr. Collins told me afterwards that his hair stood on end, and that he didn't know whether to fight or run. I felt anything but comfortable myself. I buttoned up my coat, and prepared for what seemed inevitable—a fight for my watch.

They, however, went quietly on before, and we behind. They never spoke another word, but on coming to a point where two roads met, they sheered off the direct road to London. Had I shown the least sign of hesitation or weakness they would, no doubt, have made the attempt upon which they had evidently been bent.

Six months after that I saw a copy of the *Dartford Gazette*, which contained in three columns every word of my speech. I had a meeting there subsequently in Paradise Chapel, where about 100 sat down to tea, and at the public meeting we had a hearty reception. This time a deputation was waiting to meet us, and we were accommodated in first-class style. A minister occupied the chair, and the meeting was both respectable and useful. We slept there that night, and on our road home the next morning we scattered the seeds of temperance in another place, the name of which I cannot remember. We subsequently went to Erith, and got twenty-five signatures. The meetings at Dartford have been continued ever since. Mr. Collins, who accompanied me on these two occasions, died on September 16th, 1869, after being a preacher of the Gospel for many years.

MY WORK AT MARGATE.

I was coming up from Margate about five years ago when a decent-looking man said, "Mr. McCurrey, I believe?"

"That is my name," I said, "but I don't remember you."

"But I remember you very well."

"Are you a teetotaler?"

"Yes, thank God, I am."

"Well," I said, "more people seem to know me than I know."

He said, "I have reason to remember you. My name is Ellam. You ought to be very careful, for wherever you go somebody is sure to know you."

"Well, where did you know me and when?"

"I knew you some twenty years ago, and have seen you at the bank of the Thames; but where I knew you particularly was when you had the procession from Ramsgate to Margate, and I have a bill announcing it in my possession now."

He showed this to me.

"You went with the procession," he continued, "from Ramsgate to Margate. I went down to the sands to see what the affair was like. You were the chief speaker, and I will tell you what you said. You told the people that you had been into an oven when it would bake small bread and biscuits, and you told us how you had been led astray, and how you gave up the drink. You also told us about your son, and the awful evil he fell into, and from that to this present hour I have never touched the drink. I signed the pledge shortly afterwards. I have now got a nice draper's shop of my own, and have three or four children. I am now living at Peckham, and give you a hearty invitation to come and take tea with us and address a meeting in the schoolroom there."

I have since accepted this invitation, and spoke at this meeting. I have frequently spoken on the sands at Margate, and numbers have signed the pledge.

MY WORK AT RAMSGATE.

In the early days of teetotalism we used to have very large

processions. One of these has been mentioned in connexion with Margate. At one time we had seven or eight vessels all manned by teetotalers, and belonging to the Rechabites. These vessels were not put out to fish on Sundays, but prayer-meetings were held on board. At that time there were some ten or twelve that put up the Bethel flag. The Rechabites, I should say, were very strong then, and still there is a good deal of the old leaven left. On one of the many occasions on which my voice in advocacy of teetotalism has been heard on the sands of Ramsgate a very respectable woman asked me how I was. She added, "I want to let my son see his father. He has lost his own father. Our minister knows you belong to the Bethel. Do you remember going to Dover in a fishing-boat, and we had tea on the way, and you spoke on top of a large stone; and do you remember getting them in the barracks to let you have a drum-and-fife band, and you had a meeting there?"

"Yes, I remember all that."

She just turned round, and, pointing to a great tall fellow by her side, said, "I was carrying him a little baby in my arms, and his father was drowned two years after. He said he had nothing to leave but the legacy of teetotalism which he got from you, sir."

The young fellow shook hands with me with very great warmth, and altogether I was very greatly encouraged by this little incident.

WARLEY.

I was sent down to Warley Barracks by the National Temperance League, but my style of address to the poor fellows I found there did not quite suit the authorities. I held the meeting in the large riding-school of the barracks in the presence of three non-commissioned officers, one of whom occupied the chair. I addressed them in my usual style, pointing out the advantages of total abstinence. Several of them knew me, and said, "If I had taken the pledge when I heard you ten years ago I would not have been here."

I advised them to yield implicit obedience to the officers whilst in their present position, and, further, to give up drink and save as much money as they could. In fact, the gist of my advice was to get quit of the army at the earliest possible moment. I spoke for an hour and twenty minutes, and I shall never forget the hearty way in which they shook hands with me.

For an obvious reason I was never allowed to address the Warley recruits again. When I left fifty-two had signed the pledge, and the registrar had not even then finished.

MY WORK AT BRIGHTON.

I used very often to speak on the Level at the Black Rock. Other teetotalers attempted to speak there when I left the town, but by not conciliating the authorities they were sent away. They lost their standing with the people as well as with the police. The magistrate was seen about the matter, and he said, "If you get that tall man, the builder or bricklayer, the people will hear him."

I accordingly was allowed to speak on the Level, and did so in the summer time for years and years. The last time I was there, Mr. Saunders, of Brighton, and some others, got the use of the Pavilion, where 500 poor people were entertained at tea. Mr. Saunders said that as I had been there advocating the cause for so many years I should be the principal speaker. This I accordingly was, and I had the satisfaction of knowing that a great many people signed the pledge.

POTTER'S BAR.

Though I most thoroughly appreciate the labours of temperance agents, and think them worthy of a far more substantial hire than they have ever yet got, in justice to myself I must state that I never was a professional lecturer.

Captain Trotter sent for me to address a meeting at a place called Potter's Bar, and a very wild set of fellows they were I had to talk to. They swore in a dreadful way, and one of them sent a brick flying through the window. This brick was taken by Captain Trotter to Dyrham Park, and preserved there as a curiosity. We, however, got a good number of signatures.

I have frequently elsewhere spoken of my high opinion and of the zealous and Christian labours of Captain Trotter. He never used to send me to these rough meetings by myself, but would share with me the toil and the danger. I might relate many incidents in connexion with this devoted worker, but I forbear to do so. His death was a severe blow to the temperance cause.

MEETING AT PINNER.

This meeting was held in 1839—two years after I signed the pledge—and deserves particular mention on account of some of the incidents which cluster around it. Mr. John Hull, of Uxbridge, did us very good service at that time, and was one of the most faithful friends the temperance movement ever had. In accordance with his invitation, I went down to Uxbridge in company with the Rev. James Sherman and Dr. Gorman. I went down with them in their carriage to Pinner Park to Squire Walkden, who was also a very good friend to the cause in those days. At that time we used to arrange beforehand the method in which we would address the people. The Rev. James Sherman, for instance, took the religious argument, Dr. Gorman the medical view, John Hull the moral aspect, and then I came in, as they were pleased to say, to do the practical work. We had a good dinner, though I felt in such company like a fish out of water. Subsequently we went to the meeting. They all spoke, and I came last. I told them about the oven, and it was one of the best meetings I ever had.

I was, however, rather in a fix. I had to go home that night, for if I had not done so and been at my work the next day, I should have been discharged, for I was simply a journeyman then. I said, "Gentlemen, I must go home to-night."

"No," said Mr. Sherman, "you can't. There are no means of conveyance, and besides, look how deep the snow is."

"I can't help it, sir, I must go."

"Why not stop till the morning," said the squire, "and drive back with Mr. Sherman and the doctor."

"It is impossible for me to stay."

"We ought to have let our good friend speak first, then," said the squire.

So they ought, and so they would, if I had only told them. I, however, took to the road, and a dreadful journey it turned out. I walked steadily on until I came to Harrow, and there the road lies through a churchyard. I met a man who was going in the direction of Pinner. He said, "Good morning;" and I repeated the salutation.

"Are you for London?"

"Yes."

"I am bound in the direction you have just come from. A nice morning for travelling."

"It is *very*."

And so we parted; but he told me to go through the churchyard, as it would save me a good quarter of a mile. I took his advice. When I had got half way there I heard a strange and unearthly noise, and I came at last to an open grave, which was evidently prepared to receive a corpse the next day. I came to a second open grave, but still the unaccountable and unearthly noise continued, and though none who know me will say that there is a bit of the coward about me, yet nervous excitement made the horrors of that dreadful night so depressing to my spirit that I think of it with dread even at this distance of time. The noise went "chink, chink, chink," and my hair nearly stood on end. To go back seemed almost more dreadful than to go forward, and yet to do the latter I feared might be my death. At that time the thought struck me that I had buried in that very churchyard a brother-in-law only just the Christmas before, and with the horrible fear that was creeping about my heart I began to think that if ever Satanic influence was to lead me captive at its will, it would be then. Still the "chink, chink, chink" continued, only it became more audible every moment. At last, when my fears seemed to be wrought up to the highest pitch which human nature could endure, I ascertained the cause of this strange noise. It was a milkman passing through the churchyard, and the noise was caused by the cans at his side. The circumstance may appear trifling enough, as it no doubt is, but those moments which ensued from the time when the "chinking" first became audible would comprehend the agony of a life.

"Milkman," I cried, with panting voice, "if I am not dead with fright it is no fault of yours."

"What's the matter?"

"Matter enough. Why didn't you stop the jingling of those cans?"

"Hoot, man! there's nothing to be afraid of. I wish you good morning;" and so he went on his way, the cans still going "chink, chink, chink," but no longer possessing any terror for me. My troubles were not even then over. As I was leaving the churchyard I heard the jingle of some bells, and the lowing of sheep in a pen. This, of course, was a noise that was accountable, but to my terror a huge dog suddenly, and with one loud, sharp bark, leaped into my path.

The fright was only momentary, but coming so soon after my former adventure, it was rather too much. I travelled home, and on reaching London had a cup of coffee, washed myself, and at the time appointed was working to all appearance as though the night had been passed by me in a comfortable bed, instead of in a churchyard amidst unaccountable noises, open graves, the barking of a dog, and snow that in some parts was nearly to my knees in depth.

ENFIELD.

I was frequently invited by Captain Trotter (who is now dead) to address meetings in Enfield and the neighbourhood. That gentleman will be long and affectionately remembered by the early workers. When I was ill from the effects of a fall from a high ladder, and when my eyes were bad, he came to see me, and offered me assistance. I thanked him, and said I required none; but he told me if ever I did to let him know, and I should want for nothing. When the captain became a teetotaler I took down all his boilers which he used in brewing for his family, and, instead, I made hot air-stoves and hot-houses for storing rare plants. One day when I was down there the captain called me and said, "McCurrey, do you see that brewer's dray coming up? Well, it is coming up after I have given my men money for beer."

"If it was me," I replied indignantly, "I would turn the dray back, and sack every man of them."

I was sent to Mr. Munro, of Enfield, a large potato salesman, with a letter, and told to follow his instructions. Mr. Munro got up a large meeting for me in his barn, and people came to it from all the surrounding country. A large number of persons signed the pledge, and ultimately I made a teetotal hall of the barn. I also established meetings in Enfield Chase. At the time I did this the place had acquired considerable notoriety from the fact that a sailor had been murdered there, and two men who were charged with the crime were hanged in front of the Old Bailey. Mr. Munro told me the place was a very bad one, but I resolved to hold this meeting. I went in company with a few more, and got on very well the first time. I went again, and they were rather more difficult to manage. They tried to prevent me speaking in one place, and I went to another—right opposite the public-house. The publican came out, and threatened me in the most awful way. A gentleman named Walker, who owned some property about there, came up and said, " Are they ill-using you ? "

" Not much, but they are disturbing my meeting."

Mr. Walker then said, "Yonder is my field. You can go in there out of the thoroughfare, and let your company follow you if they will."

I accordingly went into the field, but I don't know how it was, yet this murder came into my head, and I let it out as usual. I asked, "How many more men do you intend to send up to the Old Bailey to be hanged like dogs? He treated you, you robbed him of his money, and then you knocked his brains out. You are a thundering bad lot."

I felt no danger, but looked calmly into all their faces as I said this. A woman in the crowd screamed right out, and my meeting seemed to shake. It turned out that this woman was in some way connected with one of the men who was hanged. The beershop-keeper came up to me, and said, " Bricklayer !"

"Yes," I said.

"Do you know who that was ?"

"No, I don't."

"You have upset her."

"Well, I hope it will do her good."

"She is a little connected with the case you were speaking

of. How long have you been a teetotaler yourself, Mr. McCurrey?"

"Four or five years."

"I have a good mind to try it myself, for I can't do much in the beer-shop."

"Give it up then, and be a man, and turn to a respectable trade."

In about a month after the beershop-keeper came to one of the meetings, and told me that he had shut up his beer-house, opened a potato warehouse, and got on very well.

MY WORK AT BARNET.

I frequently visited Barnet, and on one or two occasions had the use of the Town Hall. I was employed by Captain Trotter for about three months in taking down his old brew-house, and putting in its place hot-air pipes to warm the house and preserve the flowers. The captain used to take me to St. Alban's, Enfield Chase, Luton, Watford, and other places, where together we strewed the seeds of teetotalism. There were no trains then, so I used to go home every Saturday on the "Blue Post" coach, which started from the corner of Tottenham Court-road. It was during that time I fell from the top of a ladder and nearly lost my sight, and it was then I had my interview with Dr. Tracey, which I have before narrated.

To resume, however. I had a great meeting in the Town Hall, Barnet, and the late lamented John Cassell was to be one of the speakers. Captain Trotter had engaged the "Welsh Bard" specially for the occasion, and had made his appearance the great feature of the evening. A crowded audience assembled to hear him, but he never came. The newspapers the next day contained an account of his arrest while drunk. John Cassell and I spoke to the people, and we managed to amuse them, but this was a great disappointment to our kind host.

HODDESDON.

Hoddesdon is a place well known for its brewing establishments. I was invited to address a meeting, and did so, but a rough one it was. We could not get in at the door at first, and when we did get in the building was so full that it would have been impossible to have packed in another individual. Attempts were made by the "baser sort" to put the lights out, and sparrows were let into the place. I sang two or three songs, as I often used to do, to quell the disturbance, and tried all I could to quiet the meeting. I said to those about me at last, "Never mind, I will go outside and take possession of one of those nine-gallon casks, and you can stand by me." I got up and spoke to those outside. I said, "Whatever you may think of me, this I know, and I can call God to witness it, that I have come here only for your good, and I don't believe there is a man in my hearing who will hurt a hair of my head. Although you get your living by brewing the accursed drink, you know that that drink makes you miserable and wretched, and you know that after the slightest injury to your physical frame you die like rotten sheep."

In the middle of all this they began to throw stones, and I got down and told them what I never told a meeting before. "If you want to do me an injury, don't unman yourselves as Englishmen. I will have a turn with the best man among you."

By this time the meeting had got into such a condition that it became dangerous to our lives, and so we betook ourselves home, our escape being favoured by the darkness. We had four signatures afterwards, one that of a barber.

Some six or eight months afterwards I went to this nice little town again! I here met this very barber, though, of course, I did not know him. He began to speak to me about teetotalism, and at last I asked, "Are you a teetotaler?"

"Thank God, I am. I would never have thrown a stone at any of you if I had known as much as I know now."

That man has prospered and got into a nice shop, with an equally nice front to it. Not only is it an "Easy Shaving Shop," but a perfumer's to boot, and altogether it is as snug an establishment as you will see in the town of Hoddesdon. At the time these events took place I had been a teetotaler some six or seven years, so that would have been about the year 1843.

When I had been a teetotaler twenty-one years, my good friends in Sydney Hall, Chelsea, gave a free tea in my honour, which I still remember with pride and satisfaction. Nearly all teetotal London was present on the occasion; and amongst the company was the son of this barber, who was now a useful, religious, and temperance missionary. Whilst upon the subject of the Sydney Hall meeting, I may add that on that occasion a good sum of money was collected to get the hall out of debt. The barber's son addressed the meeting in something very like the following strain:—

"I am a stranger to many of you, but I am not a stranger to Mr. McCurrey. I have come all the way from Hoddesdon to be present on this occasion, and I am pleased to say that the temperance work which was commenced there under such inauspicious circumstances by Mr. McCurrey so many years ago is now prospering, and a successful society is established."

He concluded by putting a guinea into the collection. I gave them five pounds, and my wife gave another five pounds, and my daughter gave something. We gathered sixty-five pounds at the meeting, and the result to the society was of lasting benefit.

A DIFFICULTY AT PADDINGTON.

I was once announced to preside at a meeting in Paddington, and a resolution was passed that it should not be opened with prayer.

"If that is your resolution," I said, "I don't preside over you."

The resolution was rescinded while I was marching to the door, and consequently I returned and resumed my appointed place. A minister opened the proceedings with prayer, and the meeting was a decided success.

BENJAMIN HATFIELD.

This man most certainly deserves to be mentioned in any record of early work in the temperance cause. He was present at the first meeting held in the Rockingham Rooms public-house, at which John Meredith, Esq., presided. I was then supposed to be just the man suitable for the audiences which used to assemble. I have often been with Mr. Meredith when he used to ring the bell and then hold a meeting. This meeting in the Rockingham Rooms was, however, a very noisy one. Mr. Hatfield on this occasion behaved very badly. I rather think I was speaking about my adventure in the oven, and some one called out, "It's a lie; no one can do that."

Hatfield got quite upset by what was said. He stood up, and I shall not soon forget the figure he cut. One of his sleeves was torn off, and a bit was out of his hat.

"How long have you been a teetotaler?" he asked.

"How long! Going on four years."

"Not a drop?"

"No; but you, I fear, have had too many drops."

"Yes," said he, "I have had too many."

"Never mind, it is a long lane that has no turning."

Somebody cried, "Turn him out!"

Whenever any one used to cry this, Mr. Meredith would say, "No, that is just the man we want." Hatfield signed the pledge, and did a great work for the temperance cause. He deserves all honour for it. So also does Mr. Meredith. It is difficult to say where the cause would have been at that time had it not been for his devoted labours. Amongst others whose names are elsewhere mentioned, I would here make special note of Mr. Jabez Inwards, Mr. T. A. Smith, and Mr. J. W. Green, who have done a work for God and temperance of which this country is to-day reaping the benefit.

CAPTAIN GEORGE PILKINGTON.

It is no easy thing in these times for a man in high social position to brave the sneers of the fashionable world by becoming an abstainer, and it was far less easy thirty-eight years ago. There were a few, however, who did so, and who, until their death, displayed a devotion worthy of the greatest of all moral reforms, which teetotalism undoubtedly was and is. Amongst these was Captain George Pilkington. Long before 1836 Captain Pilkington was working in the cause, and a life of him has been published which is a truly remarkable work. He was certainly the first I ever saw analyzing intoxicating liquors, which he did at a large meeting he convened in London. Somebody cried out, "Have mercy upon the licensed victuallers." He responded with, "Have mercy upon her Majesty's subjects."

The mantle of this great man has fallen upon one whom I mention with the greatest respect and affection—Mr. T. A. Smith. But a narrative of this kind, going back as it does into almost the earliest days of the temperance movement, would be incomplete were the name of Captain George Pilkington omitted from that small but noble army which attacked the Goliath of drink, and cast in his forehead the fatal stone of total abstinence.

[1] Died, "faithful unto death," 1874.

CHAPTER XI.

RECOGNITION OF SERVICES TO THE CAUSE.—RECOLLECTIONS OF FELLOW-WORKERS IN THE EARLY DAYS OF THE MOVEMENT.

In recording the persecutions and trials I have endured I feel that I have reason to recollect with a hundredfold more of vividness the kindnesses I have received. Friends have been won whose sympathy has soothed me in my sorrows, and encouraged me in all my efforts to do good. Unaided by human sympathy I should have sunk under the burden of many trials, but God turned the hearts of many towards me and mine, and often made my opponents and enemies to be at peace with me.

In 1840 I was presented with a handsome silver medal. The inscription on the medal runs thus:—" Presented to Mr. James McCurrey, by a few friends of the British and Foreign Temperance Society, as a testimonial of gratitude for advocating their cause.—Chelsea Temperance Hall, June 4, 1840." This was three years after I signed the pledge. The Society which presented me with this medal believed in the "long pledge" in opposition to the party then believing in the "short pledge."

PRESENTATION OF A BIBLE, ETC.

I was presented with a Bible, which contains a very nice inscription, couched in the very kindest terms, and which I much prize.

My wife, who had been ever instant in season and out of season, was, I knew, much valued, and the friends presented her with a gold ring set with diamonds. Some years ago I was presented with a watch, which I have in my possession now.

The *Weekly Record*, now better entitled the *Temperance Record*, of January 13, 1866, thus describes this interesting event in my life:—

"PRESENTATION OF A TESTIMONIAL TO MR. JAMES McCURREY.

"GREAT HALL, BROADWAY, WESTMINSTER.

"The members of the 'Choral Class' connected with this hall raised a subscription among themselves in order to present Mr. James McCurrey with a testimonial to mark their high appreciation of his valuable services. No public announcement was made of this subscription, it being confined to the Choral Class, but the amount collected being deemed sufficient, it was decided that the presentation of the testimonial should take place on Monday last, the 8th instant, when a large party of the friends and admirers of Mr. McCurrey, together with the members of the Choral Class, took tea in the large hall. After tea the public were admitted and formed a large audience. Mr. Punch was called to the chair, and opened the proceedings with some appropriate remarks. Some choice music, vocal and instrumental, was then performed, and addresses were delivered by Mr. T. A. Smith, of the National Temperance League, Mr. McBain, and Mr. Peter Johnson. Some verses composed by Mr. McSweeney, in honour of Mr. McCurrey, were read by Mr. Dinham and sung by the choir to the tune of "Auld Lang Syne." Mr. Dinham, the leader of the Choral Class, then read an address from the class to Mr. McCurrey, expressing their admiration of his consistent character and unflinching advocacy of true temperance, and begging his acceptance of the testimonial as a mark of their gratitude for the benefits they and their parents had derived from his example and teaching. Mr. Dinham then presented Mr. McCurrey with the testimonial, consisting of a beautiful, illuminated copy of the sacred Scriptures in massive binding, and also an elegant diamond ring for Mrs. McCurrey. Mr. McCurrey, in an eloquent and feeling address, returned thanks to the Choral Class for the testimonial, and said that they could not have given him anything more agreeable to his feelings than that splendid Bible. He was not in need of pecuniary assistance, but should ever prize their gift as a mark of their friendship. Some more music having been performed, Mr. Kilpatrick moved a vote of thanks to the Choral Class for presenting Mr. McCurrey with the testimonial, and in the course of his speech remarked that a few years before many of the members of the Choral Class had had medals put round their necks by Mr. McCurrey at the Band of Hope. Mr. McSweeney seconded the vote of thanks to the Choral Class, and it was carried with great applause. A vote of thanks to the chairman, and some excellent music by the Choral Class, brought the meeting to a close. The greatest enthusiasm prevailed during the proceedings, although the meeting did not terminate until near eleven o'clock."

On the week immediately after the *Weekly Record* contained the following gratifying letter:—

"SIR,—Every true teetotaler must rejoice in the expression of gratitude and veneration which was presented to that grand old man, James McCurrey, by the Westminster Choral Class.

"There is something peculiarly pleasing in this expression of feeling on the part of the young people, which reflects lasting honour on them. A few years ago many of them were children in the Westminster Band of Hope, so ably conducted by that most devoted lady Mrs. Cleaver. Often has Mr. McCurrey presided at their festivals, and as the little ones came up to receive their prizes he spoke loving words of encouragement; and now they are young men and women just entering into life, some of their number have gone to far distant lands, and when the *Record* carries the news of that happy meeting to them, and they read how their old friends at home have honoured themselves by this presentation, they will be encouraged to work harder in spreading the truths of temperance, by establishing and conducting Bands of Hope in the land of their adoption.

"Not only amongst the young has God blessed the work of His servant: many of us fathers of families in Westminster have reason to thank God that ever we heard his manly, earnest appeals. His trophies are everywhere; in many homes all over England, as the *Record* is read, thankful hearts will exclaim, 'Thank God! James McCurrey was the means of saving me and my family from misery.'

"Yours truly,
"ONE OF THE RESCUED."

It is worth the labour of a lifetime to have obtained such an epistle as this.

THE OLD WORKERS.

The old workers! What a rush of memories overwhelm me as their faces and forms rise up before me! How shall, how can I, speak in language too glowing of those men? They, with a devotion second only to that of the unlettered fishermen of old, whom they in many respects resembled, toiled day and night to sow the seeds of the movement which had blessed them, and which God, through them, was making a blessing to many. The order I mention them in here must not lead the reader to suppose that any preference is shown them, but simply as they rush into my thoughts, and are committed to paper by my amanuensis.

Mr. J. W. GREEN was a most useful man to us in the literary way. He was the editor of the *Temperance Intelligencer*.

JOHN H. ESTERBROOKE and his esteemed wife were invaluable in their respective departments. Mr. Esterbrooke was useful in the open-air movement, and then became identified with the Band of Hope movement, if, indeed, he was not its founder, so far as London is concerned.

JOHN MATHEW.—Harp Alley, in Farringdon-street, has passed away, but the memory of the good John Mathew is ineffaceable.

Mr. JOHNSTON, of Acton, who finished his career at a ripe old age, bore a noble testimony to temperance truth.

JABEZ WEST lives still, and when he dies it may with truth be said, "A prince and a great man has fallen in the temperance Israel."

WM. SPRIGGS.—The memory of Mr. Spriggs' labours will not soon be forgotten by those who knew them. Wherever the temperance cause was to be advanced there he was to be found. He knew the curse of drink, and he knew the blessings of abstinence; so that whilst teaching the people to avoid the former, he bade them embrace the latter. I was the last man who left London with him when he went on the temperance mission to Guildford, where he died.

JAMES TEARE was not a London man, though he often used to visit us. I went round London with him and Father Mathew.

WILLIAM WEST.—I should suppose that very few men have spent more money in the temperance cause than our old friend Mr. West. For far more than thirty years his has been the ready purse to help us in all our emergencies, and those, let me assure my modern teetotal friends, were not a few.

Mr. T. A. SMITH, in his early connexion with the cause, was as useful to us as a clever debater as he has latterly been as a chemical lecturer. When in future years the history of the temperance movement shall come to be written, that history will not be worth its name if it does not award a high place of merit to this devoted man.

EBENEZER WILLIAMS was a Welshman, with a warm heart, and did us good service. His mother, at eighty years of age, was so active that she danced with me on the way to Gravesend by steamer. The Rev. Dr. Marsh took me aside privately, and spoke to me on the subject. What he said had such an effect on me that I have never danced since.

GEORGE VERNEY was a second Mr. Tisdall to us, and many of the present generation have been educated under his fostering care, and at his excellent scholastic establishment at Hounslow.

JABEZ INWARDS.—Surely every teetotaler knows the devoted labours of this earnest advocate. To hear him thirty years ago was as great a treat as it is now. God bless him!

PETER CARIGAN is another of those advocates who is known

to the present generation of teetotalers for great earnestness.

The late GEORGE HOWLETT was a great assistance to us in the open-air work—that hard and perilous toil; but his constant labours are too well known to require farther mention.

The REV. FRANCIS BEARDSALL was one of the few ministers who countenanced and supported us. The hymns he composed were of the greatest service to me, especially in opening the meetings. I have named some of these elsewhere, but I may say here that I have often sung some of them for an hour at a time, to drown the storm of opposition against me.

THOMAS IRVING WHITE deserves most honourable mention. He was and is a good speaker, who never talks except as the result of deep conviction and thought. His style of advocacy was extremely useful, even in the uncouth early days.

SAMUEL CALTON, J. T. BUTEUX (whom I have before mentioned), and Mr. O'LEARY, Mr. BONIFACE, THOMAS WHITTAKER, STEPHEN GRAY, the Rev. WILLIAM BAKER, G. C. CAMPBELL (mentioned before), Dr. LOVELL, WALTER LUDBROOK, W. BRISCOMBE, BENJAMIN ROCHE, RICHARD and Mrs. GWYNNE, JOHN HILTON (with whom I delighted to work in Brighton), the Rev. H. BOURNE, WILLIAM ORPTHORPE, JOHN BOWEN, Dr. TRACEY, BRIAN HELM, Mr. DONALDSON, CHAS. HALL, CHAS. PEARMAN, and many others mentioned throughout this work, are gratefully remembered by me, as they must be by all the other living temperance men.

JOSEPH BORMOND is another highly-respected advocate. Hundreds of lectures have been given by him in Knightsbridge, near where the barracks are.

GEORGE CRUIKSHANK, that truly noble man, who, with a heroism which it is impossible too much to admire, for conscience' sake left a circle of friends which must have been very dear to him from many old associations—what shall be said of him? Who does not know his consistent life? Who does not know how he has enriched art and the temperance cause by the products of his genius? Cold and dead and unworthy of the name and mission of a temperance reformer will that man be who ever forgets the devotion of George Cruikshank to our noble cause.

The REV. DR. BURNS.—Dr. Burns was the only minister in London who stood thoroughly by us at the outset, and only recently he preached his *thirty-seventh* annual temperance sermon. We used to come from Chelsea in a body of 150 or 200 to hear him, and many reformed drunkards who, poor fellows! were afraid of the old serpent, went to his chapel to partake of the Sacrament in unfermented wine.

MR. MAGUIRE.—The Rev. Robert Maguire, the esteemed Rector of St. Olave's, Southwark, signed the pledge at a large meeting held in his late parish of Clerkenwell. He was pleased to say that it was through what I said at the meeting that caused him to do so.

The REV. W. R. BAKER was a fast friend of the temperance cause. His life was published a few years ago, and to this I would refer those of my readers who wish for full particulars on the point.

WILLIAM ORPTHORPE, of Bishopsgate-street, was a man who spent both time and money in the cause.

SAMUEL CATTON, of Plaistow, was another faithful and, I am sorry to add, persecuted labourer in the cause.

JOHN NOBLE deserves most "honourable mention" for the assistance he gave me at Brighton.

BENJAMIN ROCHE.—It was at Reading, in 1839, that I became acquainted with Squire Roche. I was sent for by Captain Trotter to address some meetings after the departure of John Hawkins, the Birmingham blacksmith, a great advocate at that time, and a faithful fellow to the end. Squire Roche was a

Middlesex magistrate and a stanch teetotaler. It was at Reading that Captain Trotter signed the pledge. It occurred in this way. The captain was down there as one of a shooting party, and, on one occasion, asked the gamekeeper if he would have anything to drink. He said, "No; I have not had any for six weeks, and I am a total abstainer." Such was the influence he had over the captain that he signed the pledge, and his sister also did the same. I am sorry to add that he was often made the victim of designing men, who came like wolves into the temperance fold for what they could get.

Rev. S. BEARDSALL died June 26th, 1842, on his way to America.

Mr. JOHN MEREDITH died in 1849. A more useful or more devoted helper to the temperance cause never lived. His sons are all teetotalers, and are worthy supporters of the cause to this day.

Mr. JOHN McLACHLAN was and is a devoted worker. That his life may long be spared should be the earnest wish of every true friend of the cause.

CAPTAIN YOUNG was another hard worker.

Mr. JOHN JOHNSTON was another faithful worker, who was identified with the Lower George-street Hall. He took charge of my open-air meeting at the end of the Suspension Bridge in 1847, and still keeps it open.

Mr. BUCKLEY, the present editor of the *Commercial World*, was a most devoted worker in early times.

EDWARD BRYAN was another true friend of the cause, when friends were few. He has been employed for twenty-nine years as foreman to Messrs. Evans and Doulton, the great pottery manufacturers of Lambeth. Some thirty years ago he asked me to address an assemblage of women who had come out of prison, and who were in a refuge provided for them by some benevolent persons at Wandsworth.

CHAPTER XII.

RECOLLECTIONS OF FATHER MATHEW AND OF SPECIAL OCCASIONS.

It has been often of late erroneously said that the introduction of temperance principles among our Irish fellow-subjects, resident in the metropolis, was when the honoured and excellent Rev. Theobald Mathew came to London in the August of 1843. Of course that event, and the great movement in Ireland associated with his name, which had preceded his coming to England, had given a great impetus to the cause; but it is simple truth to record that my friend, Mr. James Balfour, and myself convened the first temperance meeting of Roman Catholics. The Rev. Mr. Sisk, a priest at St. Mary's Roman Catholic Chapel, Chelsea, had called on Mr. Balfour, and asked him about the progress of the cause, and seemed very much impressed with some reclamations among members of the Roman Communion. He had also heard Mr. McCurrey at an open-air meeting. He said very frankly, "I know that strong drink is the besetment of our people, and their hindrance in all good things." Reflecting on this admission, Mr. Balfour waited on the priest, and obtained leave for him and myself to hold a meeting in the Roman Catholic school-room, Grove-place, New-road, on Friday, November 9, 1838. Wishing to have the meeting as effective as possible, we invited Mr. J. W. Green, Editor of the *Temperance Intelligencer*, to attend.

The Rev. Mr. Sisk was voted to the chair, and spoke very feelingly on the evils and miseries which privately came to his knowledge, or openly met his sight, through intemperance.

Mr. J. W. Green expressed the earnest desire which the new British and Foreign Temperance Society felt to have a Catholic Association in the metropolis, and he regarded that meeting as a commencement that would result in great good to the many Irish residents in London and its suburbs.

Mr. Balfour followed in a very earnest speech.

I, knowing in my business a great number of Irishmen, both journeymen and labourers, and having often seen how hard the poor fellows worked, and how madly they spent their earnings—knowing this, I followed Mr. Balfour, and at the conclusion the Rev. Chairman read the Total Abstinence pledge, submitted several rules that he had drawn up, and proposed that the meeting should be held fortnightly; and Mr. Smith, a Roman Catholic, who had long been a zealous member of the Chelsea society, was made secretary, and thirty-three signatures were obtained.

Mrs. Balfour, who was present, made a note of the following remark of Mr. Sisk's:—"The holy psalmist has said, 'Except the Lord build the house, they labour in vain that build it.' I shall expect that all who join this sober association will be examples in their more diligent observance of religious duties, and in their general deportment and conduct, so as to win others, and recommend genuine sobriety."

Mr. O'Leary, the Roman Catholic schoolmaster, a very intelligent man, during the meeting expressed himself opposed to our principles; but in a few days, after having examined the matter carefully, he signed the pledge, and became a most useful adherent. This first Roman Catholic society continued to flourish, its fortnightly meetings were well attended, and in the next year other Roman Catholic societies were formed, and thus a beginning was made, which, in a very few years, comprised numbers ready to welcome Father Mathew, and to aid him in making his progress to different districts of London.

In the present time, when as everybody must be aware, the progress of temperance has been very great amongst the Roman Catholic community, the recent action of Cardinal Manning and his clergy has given an impetus to the movement, which cannot fail to produce lasting good to the Roman Catholics of this country. I believe with one of the speakers at a recent meeting that "teetotalism will do much to remove the solitary obstacle to the greatness of the Irish people." In the light of present events, I am somewhat proud of having had the honour of speaking at the first Roman Catholic temperance meeting.

THE FATHER MATHEW MEDAL.

Father Mathew presented me with a silver medal. I went round London with him, in company with the late James Teare (this was before there were any temperance leagues, or any associations of the kind), to organize his meetings. I was presented with this medal, along with a Roman Catholic nobleman, the Earl of Arundel. The meeting at which this presentation took place was held in a large field which I had obtained from a butcher, Mr. Grant, of Chelsea. I got him and his family to be all teetotalers. At the close the Earl of Arundel shook hands with me, but I have never seen or heard of him since. Father Mathew used to call me the " Masoner." Often has he said, " Oh, Mr. McCurrey, God Almighty will bless you yet!" I went down to Enfield, and several other places with him, and got up a large number of his meetings. We both spoke in a churchyard at Bow, which was full, and I suppose a thousand signed the pledge there.

CHAPTER XIII.

LOSS OF THE COMPANION OF MY LIFE.

My narrative has shown how deep and tender was the love which bound me and my wife together. We were one in heart, in faith, and in feeling, from the time that we took each other as partners for life. Indeed, our sympathies grew stronger, if possible, as temperance opened new opportunities of usefulness. To seek and to save the lost and fallen, especially of her own sex, was an aim to which her energies were always devoted with unflagging Christian devotedness.

The loss of one who had travelled the journey of life, in sorrow and in joy, with me for nearly forty-seven years, was a grief I cannot describe and will not dwell on. Still, the certainty that she realized in the fullest degree the sweet and precious promise of our Lord, "Lo, I am with you alway, even to the end;" and that, bright as her life here was, she has gone to the brightness that knows no shadow and the joys that will not fade; while it made this life for a time very dark to me, brought heaven nearer, with the sense that she awaits me there, where there is life for evermore. These were my abiding consolations under that heavy trial.

My health, which had been perfect for many years, under the influence of grief gave symptoms of declining. A painful

MRS. MCCURREY'S MONUMENT, BROMPTON CEMETERY.

malady set in, which necessitated a severe and dangerous surgical operation. Of course, there were those who thought I ought and must take strong 'drink, but my faith in total abstinence from all intoxicants was unshaken. Through the operation, and in the long and trying recovery, I was, by God's goodness, sustained and brought again to a measure of health and strength somewhat unusual at my age.

I append a few memorials of respect for my dear Margaret's memory.

DEATH OF MY MARGARET.

The terrible event—terrible by reason of the loss I sustained, and terrible on account of the grief it produced—I cannot even now refer to without feelings of the acutest sorrow. The following tribute to her goodness and her worth appeared in the *Weekly Record* of April 7, 1866:—

"*To the Editor of the* WEEKLY RECORD.

"SIR,—The brief notice which appeared in the *Record* of the death of Mrs. James McCurrey, has called forth such a feeling of sympathy for our old and valiant champion of the temperance cause who now mourns his sad bereavement, and such a desire to know more of her who has gone to her reward, that I think it would be well if the lesson of her life were told, so that others may be encouraged and instructed by her example.

"She, alas! knew in the earlier years of her married life what it was to suffer through the intemperance of her husband; but she was a Christian woman, a praying wife and mother; and when every hope had fled, she wrestled earnestly in secret that God, in His infinite mercy, would turn the husband of her love from the errors of his ways. At length, as she always said, in answer to her prayers, she was led, in company with her husband, to attend a meeting of teetotalers held in Chelsea on the 17th of November, 1837, and there, while listening to the speaker, she thought, 'Why this is the very thing to save my husband;' and when at the close of the address the people were urged to come up and sign the pledge, she was the first to walk up to the platform and enrol her name; then, turning to her husband, she, with tears in her eyes, entreated him to follow her example. He hesitated for a minute, and then signed his name under that of his wife.

Who can tell the blessed results of that act of hers, not only on her own family, but on hundreds and thousands of others who have been reclaimed by the efforts of Mr. McCurrey? She did what she could! Would to God we could persuade other suffering wives to do as she did in this respect! She led the way.

"At that time it was not quite so easy to be a teetotaler as at present. Mrs. McCurrey from the first day boldly avowed her principles as a thorough teetotaler, and at once commenced to work earnestly. Paying no attention to the laughs and jeers of her neighbours, she was to be seen night after night assisting at the meetings; now encouraging some poor, forlorn outcast of her own sex to give up the destroying drink; now urging some suffering wife to do as she had done by signing the pledge for her husband's sake; now standing at the door with a lamp in one hand, and temperance papers in the other, offering them for sale to the people as they came in; in everything, in season and out of season, doing all that became a Christian woman to help on the cause of teetotalism. Often did she leave her home to visit the abodes of sin and misery. Blessings followed her pious labours; her presence made sunshine in many a dark home and heart. She was the Miss Nightingale of the early years of teetotalism in Chelsea. When her husband first attempted to speak in public she encouraged him to go on. Often when he returned disheartened she inspired him with courage to go forth in the strength of God to fight like a man for the truths of temperance. No one knows how much of the success which has attended the efforts of Mr. McCurrey was due to the influence of his dear partner in life. She was unknown to the world, but her memory will be cherished very dearly not only by her own sorrowing family, but by those who have been rescued by the blessing of God on her humble endeavours. The lesson of her quiet heroism is with us. She has gone to her reward, and truly her works do follow her. She is now enjoying the immediate presence of Him who has said, 'Inasmuch as ye did it to the least of these, ye did it unto Me; enter thou into the joy of thy Lord.'

"Yours very truly,

"ONE OF THE RESCUED."

LETTER FROM MRS. BALFOUR.

"DEAR FRIEND,—Among the earliest of my recollections of the temperance cause is the energetic open-air speaking of yourself, and the constant devotedness of your dear wife.

"It was up-hill work in those early days (1837-8), and among the plans of usefulness we devised to spread our principles was the formation of a Female Temperance Society. On the first Committee of that Society (to which I also belonged) Mrs. McCurrey was an esteemed and active member. I recollect that little gathering of zealous women with affection. Our aims were so great, our means so small.

"There was one subject on which Mrs. McCurrey and I always thought and felt alike. We held it the bounden duty of a wife to help her husband in treading the new, and to many a man difficult, path of sobriety. Mrs. McCurrey had not for a moment hesitated in her own course, nor had I. Our simple maxim was, 'If we are to expect men in the midst of toil and temptation to give up a great deal, surely we wives and mothers can give up a little.' On this plan we had both acted. Wherever our husbands might be tempted we resolved it should not be at their own fireside. Particularly were we desirous that our rescued members, over whom as a Society we rejoiced with trembling, should have helpers, not hinderers, in their homes. Nothing pained or surprised us more than to find the wife of some rescued inebriate still clinging to the delusion—the selfish prejudice rather—that she must have her half-pint, or her little drop.

"Many a mile has Mrs. McCurrey walked to see, and many an earnest entreaty has she uttered to the wives, to have mercy on themselves, their husbands, and their children, and to set them an unmistakeably sober example. I well recollect calling with her on a young wife in good circumstances, who lived in Simmonds-street, Chelsea, and whose husband, tottering on the brink of intemperance, had signed at our Temperance Room, in the King's-road (before we had the Temperance Hall). The reply she made to all our entreaties was, 'I take so little, I have no need to give it up; I couldn't live without it.' 'You sit here, at home,' we said, 'among your little children, secure from temptation; your husband goes out on his business, and is tempted at every turn. It is, and must be, hard for him to resist. You say you fear he loves it, and that he spends more than he should, and you dread the future, and yet you will not give up your sips; you even say you cannot; how can you possibly expect him to abstain?'

"Mrs. McCurrey reasoned until the tears streamed down her cheeks, and we had to leave foiled by the senseless words, 'I take so little.'

"When we got outside, I recollect taking Mrs. McCurrey's hands and clasping them in mine, and saying, as we both wept, 'Neither would they believe though one rose from the dead.' 'Ah!' she said, 'it's hard; it's hard, that we can make no impression; but it's harder for that poor thing.'

"The result proved so, for that man soon broke his pledge, then deserted his wife; and when, two years after, I saw that young woman again, she was waiting among a wretched group to receive a dole of bread at the workhouse door!

"I can fully understand how such a wife must be missed by you, for she supplemented all your temperance labours, and in her genial way was a missionary to the wives of our reclaimed men, and those women, always the most difficult to restore, who had contracted a love for strong drink.

"Removal to a north-western suburb of London in 1841 prevented my seeing much of your dear wife for many years. I heard of her, and always with interest and esteem, and the full assurance that though we rarely met we were both occupied in His service who does not despise feeble efforts, and often makes the weak things of this world confound the mighty.

"She has gone before to her heavenly rest; may we also be faithful unto death, and so gain the crown of life.

"Yours most truly,

"C. L. BALFOUR."

CHAPTER XIV.

CONCLUSION.—THE EVENING OF LIFE.

"Knowledge by suffering entereth,
And life is perfected by death."

How small in the retrospect seems the amount of even a long life's work! I feel as I see the gin-palaces flaring, and the public-houses full, and hear of the wealth of brewers and distillers, and the increase of crimes of violence, and of female intemperance, as if, after all, I and my temperance friends have done nothing; yet this is, I know, a mere passing depression. We, a mere handful of humble men, attacked the most popular delusion, the most seductive vice, the established national sin, supported by ages of false teaching and practice, and by all the aids and sanction that luxury, self-indulgence, and appetite could bring to promote it, to say nothing of the sordid motives and wealth involved in it. Our only weapons were truth and energy, but of money or human power in the outset we had none. The pioneers of the temperance cause were mostly rough men, strong only in the sense of right, and the belief that God would make them powerful, even to the pulling down of the strongholds of Satan. And in little more than forty years the total abstinence principle has spread over and is known throughout the whole Christian world. It numbers its hundreds of thousands of adherents, and is admitted to be (even by our adversaries) the only remedy to reclaim the fallen, and the safest preventive from falling. People confess its merits for the young, and opponents must and do rejoice to see our Bands of Hope, and own the value of the organization of the Good Templar Societies, which have grown out of our old Temperance Societies, as flowers spring from a root, or fruit ripens on a tree. Yet, while these admissions are made, certain it is that many who think it very good for others will not try it themselves, and hence the drinking customs are perpetuated, and our efforts foiled. As an eminent physician has said, " Perhaps there is not *one* case of illness in twenty in which stimulants are required, but most patients think they themselves are that special *one.*" With the increase of wealth, and the higher wages, and shorter hours of toil, all great advantages which might be made great blessings, there has come an increase of temptation. The sale of intoxicants at grocers and pastrycooks has terribly increased the opportunities for female intemperance; many who would shrink from going or sending to the publican, go or send to the grocers readily. Then there are the weak, the unthinking, and the young; these are easily led to take the drink which is offered at all refreshment counters, in places of amusement, and on railway platforms, so that our work of reform is obstructed, and our efforts hindered. These are our discouragements. Yet, amid all, it is gratifying to know that a society which could not thirty years ago obtain without great difficulty a poor school-room or humble building to meet in, and was mostly sneered at by ministers of religion, now numbers its friends among the leading clergymen and ministers of the Church of England, and has been proclaimed within the walls of Westminster Abbey, and from the most celebrated pulpits in the land. "What hath God wrought!" is naturally my exclamation.

THE QUEEN AND THE TEMPERANCE MOVEMENT.

The Rev. Basil Wilberforce, son of the late Bishop of Winchester, and rector of St. Mary's, in Southampton, having recently placed in the hands of her Majesty certain publications connected with the temperance movement, has received the following gracious reply through Sir Thomas Biddulph, indicating her Majesty's interest in the movement :—

"I am desired to thank you for placing in her Majesty's hands works on a subject of the deepest importance to her and to every one in this country. It is impossible for the Queen not to be grateful to those who endeavour to mitigate an evil of such magnitude as the widely-spread intemperance which unfortunately prevails."

The formation of the Temperance Building Society is a fact I look back upon with the greatest satisfaction. I and some of my old friends were the founders of this institution, and have been its managing directors for upwards of twenty-one years. Hundreds of men have, by the aid of this society, obtained their own houses, and instead of paying rent to others have become their own landlords, and obtained their social independence and political influence. Upwards of a million of money has passed through the Temperance Building Society, and the institution has been most successful.

The medical profession, which in former times so greatly opposed us, now repeats and enforces our arguments. We have eminent surgeons, physicians, professors of physiology, chemists, and men of science on our side. A Temperance Hospital has been founded, and has hitherto carried out our principles with remarkable success; while scientific journals and writers have reconsidered the whole subject of alcoholics, and reversed, to a very great extent, the practices of former times. I bless God that I have been permitted to see this change. Amid much to discourage one so ardent as I am and so earnest to overthrow the drinking system, there remains much to fill me with wonder and gratitude. My experience, as age gathers upon me, is that my mind continues clear; my strength, after all that has passed to try it, remains wonderful. I can yet walk miles to a meeting, speak without any extra fatigue, and feel all my sympathies fresh and active in the cause of suffering humanity.

A friend of my dear Margaret's, who had been her kind attendant in her last illness, and who was a family connexion through the marriage of my son Robert, in course of time became my second wife; so that I am not lonely, and the remnant of my days will, I trust, by the mercy of my Saviour, be spent in His service while I can work, and ever in His love, when working has to be exchanged for waiting.

It has pleased God to chasten me; my children are all gone; but I can, with perfect resignation, say, "The Lord gave and the Lord hath taken away, blessed be the name of the Lord." My life has had its clouds and storms, but the Lord has been and is my refuge and strength; and now, in my evening hours, He has given me competence, faithful friends, a kind home companion, and, far above all, through faith in Christ, that peace which passeth all understanding, in which condition I humbly wait His summons.

> " Here I raise my Ebenezer,
>   Hither by God's help I've come,
> And I hope by His good pleasure,
>   Safely to arrive at home."

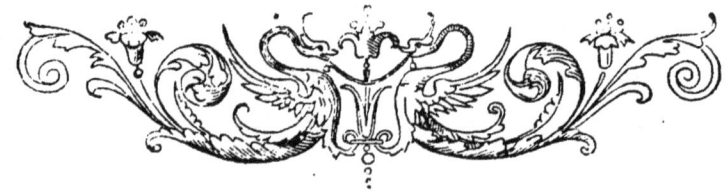

GILBERT AND RIVINGTON, PRINTERS, ST. JOHN'S SQUARE, LONDON.

ILLUSTRATED PUBLICATIONS
ISSUED BY
MESSRS. S. W. PARTRIDGE & CO.,
9, PATERNOSTER ROW, LONDON.

FOR SUNDAY & DAY SCHOOLS, LIBRARIES, ETC.

One Hundred Hieroglyphic Bible Readings for the Young. Cloth, Gilt Edges, 5s.

The Babes in the Basket; or, Daph and her Charge. Cloth, 2s. 6d.

Ben's Boyhood. By Mrs. Bowen. Cloth plain, 2s. 6d.

Illustrated Anecdotes and Pithy Pieces of Prose and Verse. Compiled by T. B. S. With numerous Illustrations. Cloth Plain, 2s. 6d.

Leaves from the Tree of Life. By Rev. R. Newton, D.D. With numerous Illustrations. Cloth, 2s. 6d.

Nature's Mighty Wonders. By Dr. Newton. Cloth, 2s. 6d,

The Best Things. By Rev. Dr. Newton. With numerous illustrations. Cloth, 2s. 6d.

The Safe Compass and How it Points. By Rev. Dr. Newton. With numerous Illustrations. Cloth, 2s. 6d

Anecdotes of the Aborigines; Historical and Missionary. Cloth, 1s. 6d.

Bible Jewels. By Dr. Newton. Cloth, 1s. 6d.

Bible Wonders. By Rev. Dr. Newton. Cloth, 1s. 6d.

The Dairyman's Daughter. By the Rev. Legh Richmond, M.A. Cloth, 1s. 6d.; Gilt, 2s. 6d.

Domestic Addresses. By Old Humphrey. Cloth 1s. 6d.

Every day Lessons. By Old Humphrey. Cloth 1s. 6d.

Family Walking Sticks; or Prose Portraits of my Relations. By Old Humphrey, with a Preface by his Widow. Cloth, 1s. 6d.

The Great Pilot and His Lessons. By the Author of "The Giants, and how to Fight Them." Cloth, 1s. 6d.

The History of King Solomon. By Mrs. M. A. Hallock. With numerous Illustrations. Cloth, 1s. 6d.

Illustrated Sabbath Facts: or, God's Weekly Gift to the Weary. Reprinted from the "British Workman." Cloth, 1s. 6d.

A Kiss for a Blow; or, a Collection of Stories for Children. By Henry C. Wright. Cloth, 1s. 6d.

The Little Woodman and his dog Cæsar. By Mrs. Sherwood. Cloth, 1s. 6d.; Gilt, 2s. 6d.

"Puffing Billy" and the Prize "Rocket;" or, the Story of the Stephensons and our Railways. By Mrs. H. C. Knight. Cloth plain, 1s. 6d.

Rills from the Fountain of Life. By Dr. Newton. Cloth, 1s. 6d.

Sketches from my Note-Book. By Old Humphrey. Cloth, 1s. 6d.

Sunday School Illustrations. By Ephraim Holding (Old Humphrey). Cloth 1s. 6d.

Children and Jesus; or, Stories to Children about Jesus. By Rev. E. P. Hammond. Cloth, 1s.

Divine and Moral Songs. By Dr. Watts. Cloth, 1s.

The Giants; and How to Fight Them, By Dr. Newton. Cloth, 1s.

Jenny's Geranium; or, the Prize Flower of a London Court. Cloth, 1s

A Mother's Stories for her Children. By the late Mrs. Carus Wilson. Cloth, 1s.

Rachel; or, Little Faults. By Charlotte Elizabeth. Cloth 1s.

The Story of Little Alfred. By D. J. E., Author of "Story of the Lost 'London.'" Cloth, 1s.

Thoughts for Young Thinkers. By Aaron Hall (Old Humphrey). Cloth, 1s.

Toil and Trust; or, Life Story of Patty, the Workhouse Girl. By Mrs. Balfour. Cloth, 1s.

Widow Green and her Three Nieces. By Mrs. Ellis. Cloth, 1s.

Bible Texts. In two packets (A & B) with coloured covers, containing fifty assorted texts in each, price 6d. each packet.

The Bible the Book for all. By Jacob Post. Cloth, 6d.

Little Sermons for Little People. By William Locke. Cloth, 6d.

TEMPERANCE.

(Many of these are suitable for Sunday School Libraries.)

A Bunch of Cherries, Gathered and Strung by J. W. Kirton Esq., Author of "Buy your own Cherries. Cloth 3s. 6d.

Three Opportunities; or, Story of Henry Forrester. Cloth. 2s. 6d.

The Four Pillars of Temperance. By the Author of "Buy your own Cherries." Paper Boards, 1s.; Cloth, 1s. 6d.

Illustrated Temperance Anecdotes; or, Facts and Figures for the Platform and the People. Compiled by the Editor of the "British Workman." 1st and 2nd series. Cloth, 1s. 6d. each.

The Mysterious Parchment; an American Story. Edited by J. W. Kirton, Author of "Buy your own Cherries." Cloth, 1s. 6d.

Church of England Temperance Tracts. Illustrated. Assorted packets, 1s.

Club Night: a Village Record. By Mrs. C. L. Balfour. Cloth, 1s.

Come Home, Mother! A Story for Mothers. Cloth, 1s.

Cousin Bessie: a Story of Youthful Earnestness. Cloth, 1s.

Digging a Grave with a Wine Glass. By Mrs. S. C. Hall. Cloth, 1s.

Frank Spencer's Rule of Life. By J. W. Kirton, Author of "Buy your own Cherries." Cloth, 1s.

The Haunted House; or Dark Passages in the Life of Dora Langley. By Eliza S. Oldham. Cloth, 1s.

How to Stop Drunkenness. By Charles Buxton, Esq., M.P. Cloth, 1s.

John Heppel; or, "Just One Glass." Cloth, 1s.

John Todd, and how he Stirred his own Broth-Pot. Cloth, 1s.

Nothing Like Example. By Nelsie Brook. With Engravings. Cloth, 1s.

Parish Difficulty and its Remedy. By K. Ashley. Cloth, 1s.

Passages in the History of a Shilling. By Mrs. C. L. Balfour. Cloth, 1s.

The Temperance Manual. By the Rev. Justin Edwards, D.D. Cloth, 1s.

Two Christmas Days; and the Christmas-Box. Cloth, 1s.

Wanderings of a Bible, and My Mother's Bible. Cloth, 1s.

"Buy your own Cherries." Prose Edition. By J. W. Kirton, Esq. Cloth, 6d.

"Buy your own Cherries." Versified from the Original Edition. Cloth, 6d.

Christopher Thorpe's Victory. A Tale for the Upper Classes. By Nelsie Brook. Cloth, 6d.

John Worth; or, The Drunkard's Death. Cloth, 6d.

Pastor's Pledge of Total Abstinence. By Rev. William Roaf. 6d.

Right Opposite. A Tale by Lucius M. Sargent. Cloth, 6d.

Tottie's Christmas Shoes. By Nelsie Brook. Cover printed in colours, 6d.

Wanderers Reclaimed; or, Truth Stranger than Fiction. 3d.

History and Mystery of a Glass of Ale. By the Author of "Buy your own Cherries." 2d.

"Good Fruit." With cover, 2d.

"He Drinks." With cover, 2d.

"Not a Drop More, Daniel." With coloured cover, 2d.

William and Mary; or, The Fatal Blow. By Mrs. Ellis. 2d.

Clergyman's Reasons for Teetotalism. 1d.

Family Pledge Card. 1d.

Total Abstinence from Alcoholic or Intoxicating Drinks, Safe, Legitimate, and Expedient. 1d.

What are Bands of Hope; and How to Form Them 1d.

KINDNESS TO ANIMALS, ETC.

Animals and their Young. By Harland Coultas. With Full-page Engravings. Cloth, 5s.

Animal Sagacity; or, Remarkable Incidents Illustrative of the Sagacity of Animals. By Mrs. S. C. Hall. Cloth, 5s.; Extra Gilt, 7s. 6d.

Anecdotes in Natural History. By the Rev. F. O. Morris, B.A. Cloth, 5s.

Birds and their Nests. By Mary Howitt. Cloth, 5s.

Clever Dogs, Horses, &c., with Anecdotes of other Animals. By Shirley Hibberd, Esq. Cloth, 5s.; Gilt, 7s. 6d.

Dogs and their Doings. By Rev. F. O. Morris, B.A. Cloth, 5s.; Gilt Edges, 7s. 6d.

Natural History Stories for my Juvenile Friends. By Mary Howitt. Containing interesting accounts of Natural History subjects, and full-page illustrations. Cloth, 5s.

Our Children's Pets; being Stories about Animals in Prose and Verse. By Josephine. Cloth, 5s.; Gilt, 7s. 6d.

Our Dumb Companions; or, Stories about Dogs, Horses, Cats, and Donkeys. By Rev. T. Jackson, M.A. Cloth, 5s.; Gilt, 7s. 6d.

Our Dumb Neighbours; or, Conversations of a Father with his Children on Domestic and other Animals. Intended as a Sequel to "Our Dumb Companions." By Rev. T. Jackson, M.A. Cloth, 5s.; Gilt, 7s. 6d.

Our Feathered Companions, Neighbours, and Visitors. By Rev. T. Jackson, M.A. Cloth, 5s.; Gilt Edges, 7s. 6d.

Our Four-footed Friends; or, the History of Manor Farm, and the People and Animals there. By Mary Howitt. Cloth, medallion on side, 5s.

Our Zoological Friends. By Professor Harland Coultas. Being a short account, with engravings, of Animals. Cloth, 6s.

Natural History Picture Roll. Consisting of 31 Illustrated Leaves, with simple large type Letterpress, suitable to hang up in the Nursery, Schoolroom, etc. Price 3s.

Our Duty to Animals. By Mrs. C. Bray, Author of "Physiology for Schools," &c. Intended to teach the young kindness to animals. Cloth, 1s. 6d; Limp, 1s.

A Mother's Lessons on Kindness to Animals. 1st, 2nd, and 3rd Series, Cloth 1s.; Limp, 6d. each.

Claims of Animals. A Lecture on the duty of promoting kindness to the Animal Creation. In large type, with Illustrations. Cloth, 1s. Commended to the notice of Schoolmasters.

Dick and his Donkey; or, How to Pay the Rent. Cloth, 6d.

Little Fan. Cloth, 6d.

Only a Ladybird. Cloth, 6d.

Richard Barton; or, The Wounded Bird. Cloth, 6d.

A Few Words on a Neglected Subject. By Mary Howitt. 3d.

Old Janet's Christmas Gift. An interesting Story of a Donkey. Coloured cover, 2d.

Old Oscar, the Faithful Dog. By H. G. Reid. 2d.

Anecdotes of Animals. With Cover and full of Illustrations. 1d. each.
1. Anecdotes of Horses.
2. Anecdotes of Dogs.
3. Anecdotes of Donkeys.
4. Neddy and Me.
5. Blackbird's Nest.

Animals' Friend Sheet Almanac. Published annually. With costly engravings and letterpress. 1d.

Halfpenny Books, for
Circulation in Schools.
- Mercy to Animals.
- Plea for the Ill-used Donkey
- Birds and their Nests.
- Only for Fun.
- Lessons on Kindness.
- The Two Nests.
- Anecdotes of Little Dogs.
- The Bird's Nest.
- Lessons on Kindness.
- Spring Flowers and Birds.
- True Duncan; or, Poor Little Tabby.
- Little Frank and Old Dobbin.

Illustrated Fly Leaves.
2s. 6d. per 100.
No. 87. A Plea for the Birds.

Illustrated Wall-papers.
1d. each.
- No. 11. A Plea for the Donkey
- ,, 23. A Plea for the Birds
- ,, 38. Horses and their Masters
- ,, 51. The Shoeing Forge
- ,, 52. Robin and the Railway Guard
- ,, 59. How to Manage Horses
- ,, 68. Our Little Feathered Friends
- ,, 72. The Cow's Complaint
- ,, 73. Man's Noble Friend — The Horse
- ,, 74. A Royal Society
- ,, 77. The Costermonger

Juvenile Pictorial Gallery.
1d. each.
- No. 2. The Little Wren
- ,, 14. Elijah and the Ravens
- ,, 15. The Zebra
- ,, 16. The Cow and Calf
- ,, 17. The Goose
- ,, 19. The Early Riser
- ,, 20. Duck and Ducklings
- ,, 21. The Yak
- ,, 24. The Sloth
- ,, 25. The Peacock
- ,, 26. The Nightingale
- ,, 27. The Quail.

Cabman's Cat. By Mrs. S. C. Hall. One Halfpenny.

Cure for Moths. One Halfpenny.

SOLDIERS & SAILORS.

John Hobbs: a Temperance Tale of British India. Cloth, 1s.

Out at Sea: A few Simple Ballads addressed to Sailors. Cloth, 1s. An Edition in paper covers, 6d.

Ben and his Mother. By Mrs. Carus Wilson. Cloth, 6d.

Articles of War: A Dialogue between Two Soldiers. 3d.

Ned Stokes, the Man-o'-War's-Man. By Agnes E. Weston. 3d.

Soldier's Testimony. Gilt edges. 3d.

"He Drinks!" With cover, 2d.

"The Drummer Boy." With cover, 2d.

Does it Answer? 1d.

For French Soldiers and Sailors, &c. Nos. 1 to 12 of the "British Workman" in French. 1d. each.

For Italian Soldiers, &c. Nos. 1 to 4 of the "British Workman" in Italian. 1d. each.

For Norwegian Sailors, &c. Nos. 1 and 2 of the "British Workman" in Norse. 1d. each.

For Portuguese Sailors, &c. No. 1 of the "British Workman" in Portuguese. 1d.

For Spanish Sailors and Soldiers, &c. Nos. 1 to 15 of the "British Workman" in Spanish. 1d. each. Nos. 1 to 12 in one vol., 1s. 6d.

FOR WORKING MEN.
(See also *Temperance*, etc.)

Happy Half-hours. Being Ten Readings for Working Men, bound up in one volume. By various Authors. Cloth, 3s.

Illustrated Penny Readings: being Twelve Separate Readings in each Series, by various Authors. In Packets or Paper Covers. First, Second, and Third Series, 1s. each; cloth, 1s. 6d.

Sparks from the Anvil. By Elihu Burritt. Cloth, 1s. 6d.

Never Give Up. A Christmas Story for Working Men and their Wives. By Nelsie Brook. Cloth, 1s.

Nothing Like Example. By Nelsie Brook. With engravings. Cloth, 1s.

Rainy Days and How to Meet Them. By Mrs. Marshall. Cloth, 1s.

Tom Burton: A Tale of the Workshop. By the Author of "The Working Man's Way in the World." Cloth, 1s.

The Best Master; or, Can Coachmen have their Sundays? By the Author of "Household Proverbs." Cloth, 6d.

"Buy Your Own Cherries." By J. W. Kirton, Esq. Cloth, 6d.

Illustrated Handbills, for General Distribution. Containing One Hundred Handbills, assorted, on Temperance, Kindness to Animals, for Promoting the Better Observance of the Lord's Day, Gospel Narrative, &c. Sixpenny packets.

Lost in the Snow; or, The Kentish Fisherman. By Mrs. C. Rigg. With numerous Illustrations, Cloth, 6d.

Farmer Ellicot; or, Begin and End with God. 3d.

John Jarvis, the Reformed Hatter. 3d.

Uncle David's Advice to Young Men and Young Women on Marriage. 3d.

Uncle David's Visit to a New-Married Wife, and the Counsels he gave her. 3d.

"British Workman" Series of Tracts. Intended for circulation amongst the Working Classes. 2d. each.
1. Darby Brill
2. The Carpenter's Speech
3. The Swearing Parrot
4. Tom Carter's Way of Doing Good
5. The Last Customer
6. John Harding's Locket
7. "Right about Face"
8. Going Aloft
9. He Drinks
10. Doing his Duty
11. Good Fruit
12. The Bent Shilling
13. The Drummer Boy
14. Inch Auger
15. Split Navvy
16. Put on the Break Jim
17. Taking up of Barney O'Rourke
18. The House that John Built
19. Articles of War
20. Little Sam Groves.

Coloured Tracts. Twenty pages. With Coloured Cover. 2d. each.
1. Buy your own Cherries
2. Matthew Hart's Dream
3. Old Janet's Christmas Gift
4. A Little Child shall lead Them
5. The Last Penny
6. Out of Work
7. John Stepping Forth
8. The Independent Labourer
9. Bought with a Price. By A. L. O. E.
10. Bethlehem
11. The Three Bags of Gold.
12. The Hidden Foe, By A. L. O. E
13. No Work No Bread
14. Light in the Bars
15. Tramp's Story
16. Thady O'Connor
17. The Shadow on the Door
18. Fisherman's Shagreen Box
19. Going Down Hill
20. Not a Drop more Daniel
21. Mike Slattery
22. The Holly Boy
23. Melodious Mat

Nos. 1 to 10 bound in one volume Cloth plain, 3s.

"It's Nobbut," and "Nivver Heed." By Robert Baker, Esq., Inspector of Factories. 2d.

Work and Wages. By J. W. Kirton, Author of "Buy your own Cherries." 2d.

Illustrated Penny Readings:—
1. Who's your Friend?
2. Autobiography of a Reformed Thief
3. What happened to Joe Barker
4. The Losings' Bank
5. The Plank will Bear
6. Take care of your "Tis Buts"
7. The Market Pint
8. The Shabby Surtout
9. The Wonder-Working Bedstead
10. My Account with Her Majesty
11. The Wounded Stag
12. The Temperance Life-boat Crew
13. Polly Pratt's Secret for making £5 Notes
14. The Life-belt
15. Crippled Jenny; or, the Voice of Flowers
16. The Doings of Drink
17. How Sam Adams' Pipe became a Pig
18. The Sunday Excursion Train
19. The First and Last Tiff
20. Frank's Sunday Coat; or, The Sabbath kept Holy
21. The King's Messenger
22. Parley the Porter
23. Fred Harford's First Great Coat
24. Help-myself Society
25. The Cabman's Holiday

26. Buy your own Goose
27. Horses and their Masters
28. The Gin Shop. Twelve Plates
29. Seed-time and Harvest
30. Build your own House
31. On Looking Seedy
32. Cobbler's Blackbird
33. Buy your own Cherries. Prose
34. Buy your own Cherries. Verse
35. Building a House with a Teacup
36. For the Good of the House
37. The Woman's Crusade

Nos. 1 to 36 in 3 vols., done up in Cloth, 1s. 6d. each; Paper Boards, 1s. each; Packets 1s. each.

Illustrated Wall Papers.

Reprints in large type from the "British Workman." For the Walls of Workshops and Schools, Ships' Cabins, Barbers' Shops, &c. One Penny each. And done up in One Shilling packets, containing twelve numbers. Five Shilling packets, containing Nos. 1 to 60.

1. "No Swearing Allowed"
2. Bob, the Cabin Boy
3. "Swallowing a Yard of Land"
4. "Knock off those Chains"
5. "He stands Fire!"
6. Fisherman and Porter
7. "Will Father be a Goat?"
8. Man with a Cross on his Back
9. John Maynard, the Brave Pilot
10. My Account with Her Majesty
11. A Plea for the Donkey
12. Preparing for the Flower Show
13. Gin Shop.
14. Thomas Paine's Recantation
15. Oil and Stewed Eels
16. The Blue Jacket's Sampler
17. Buy your own Cherries
18. Fred Harford's Great Coat
19. Reduced to the Ranks
20. Musical Coal Man
21. The Fool's Pence
22. "What's that to Me?"
23. A Plea for the Birds
24. A Pledge for a Pledge
25. The First Snowdrop
26. The Losings' Bank and the Savings Bank
27. Mike Donovan's Looking Glass
28. John Morton's New Harmonium
29. On the Look-Out
30. The "Tis Buts," Box
31. The Prodigal Son
32. The Christmas Arm Chair
33. The Village Gleaner
34. The Ambitious Blacksmith
35. My First Ministerial Difficulty
36. Something to Show for your Money
37. Stop! Mend your Buckle
38. Horses and their Masters
39. The Parable of the Sower
40. Jack and the Yellow Boys
41. The Christmas Sheaf
42. Discontented Pendulum
43. The Life Boat
44. Providence will Provide
45. Celebrated Italians
46. Dust Ho!
47. A Plea for Washerwomen
48. The Nativity
49. The Name in Gold Letters
50. John Rose's Freehold
51. The Shoeing Forge
52. Robin and Railway Guard
53. In the Far Country
54. Canute's Rebuke
55. Tom Carter's way of Doing Good
56. The Two Gardeners
57. Dip your Roll in your own Pot
58. Our Christmas Tree
59. How to Manage Horses
60. Home-Coming of Darby Brill
61. Scripture Patchwork Quilt
62. Michael Donovan
63. "That's Thee, Jem"
64. The Secret of England's Greatness
65. My Uncle's Life Motto
66. Should Museums be opened on Sundays?
67. Where are you going, Thomas Brown?
68. Our Little Feathered Friends
69. Tim's Oration
70. Live and Let Live
71. The Story of a Violin
72. The Cow's Complaint
73. Man's Noble Friend—The Horse
74. A Royal Society
75. Hints for Working Men.
76. The Well to-do Cabman
77. The Costermonger

Jeffrey the Murderer.
By the Rev. G. W. McCree. 1d.

Providence Row; or, The
Successful Collier. By Rev. T. H. Walker. 1d.

Slavery in England. A
Vision of the Night. 1d.

Sunday on "The Line;"
or, Plain Facts for Working Men. 1d.

"British Workman"
Placards. Adapted for Workshops, &c. 1d.; coloured, 3d. each. Nos. 1 to 14. Nos. 1 to 12 done up in Packets, 1s. If an order be sent with 14 stamps, the Complete Set will be forwarded post free.

Readings for the Dinner
Hour; Good Advice for Working Men, etc. Printed on toned paper, 8pp. One halfpenny each.

1. The Silver Staff: or, Help for Old Age
2. In the Same Boat
3. The Confession. By Mrs. Balfour
4. Buy your own Cherries
5. Poor Man's House Repaired
6. Only Once
7. Strike; a Little Comedy
8. John Jarvis
9. My Mother's Gold Ring
10. Home-coming of Darby Brill

11. Fred Harford's Great Coat
12. Ben Starkey's Strike
13. Bob the Cabin-boy
14. Old Tim, the Singing Cobbler
15. The Worsted Stocking
16. Maggie Dean's Pleading.

HOME AND FOREIGN MISSIONS.

Anecdotes of the Aborigines: Historical and Missionary. Cloth 1s. 6d.

Roger Miller; or, Heroism in Humble Life. Cloth, 1s. 6d.

Brands Plucked from the Burning. By the Rev. J. H. Wilson. Cloth, 1s.

Friends of the Friendless; or, a Few Chapters from Prison Life. By Mrs. Balfour. Cloth, 6d.

Scrub, the Workhouse Boy. By Mrs. Balfour. 6d.

BOOKS FOR BOYS.
(See also Temperance, etc.)

Jack the Conqueror; or, Difficulties Overcome. By the Author of "Dick and his Donkey." Cloth, 5s.

Ben's Boyhood. By the Author of "Dick and his Donkey." Cloth, 2s. 6d.

Ellerslie House: A Book for Boys. By Emma Leslie. Cloth, 2s. 6d.

A Golden Year; and its Lessons of Labour. Cloth, 2s. 6d.

The Natural History of the Year. By the late B. B. Woodward, Esq., B.A., Librarian to the Queen. 2s. 6d.

The Little Woodman and his Dog Cæsar. By Mrs Sherwood Cloth, 1s. 6d.; gilt, 2s. 6d.

"Puffing Billy" and the Prize "Rocket;" or, the Story of the Stephensons and our Railways. By Mrs. H. C. Knight, Cloth, plain, 1s. 6d.

Vignettes of American History. By Mary Howitt. Cloth, 1s. 6d.

Frank Spencer's Rule of Life. By J. W. Kirton, Author of "Buy your own Cherries." Cloth, 1s.

No Gains without Pains: a True Story. By H. C. Knight. Cloth, 1s.

Willy Heath and the House Rent. By William Leask, D.D. Cloth, 1s.

Ernest Clarke's Fall; or, Lead us not into Temptation. Cloth, 6d.

How Tom Tomkins Made his Fortune. Cloth, 6d.

Joseph Selden, the Cripple; or, an Angel in our Home. By the Author of "The Dalrymples." Cloth, 6d.

Philip Markham's Two Lessons. By the Author of "Dick and his Donkey." Cloth, 6d.

Story of Two Apprentices; The Dishonest and the Successful. By the Rev. J. T. Barr. Cloth, 6d.

The Tiny Library. Books printed in large type. Cloth, 6d.
1. Hot Coals
2. The Golden Rule
3. Grandpapa's Walking Stick
4. Honesty the Best Policy
5. Silver Cup
6. Short Stories
7. Brave Little Boys
8. Ben and His Mother
9. Little David
10. Richard Barton; or the Wounded Bird
11. Little Jim, the Rag Merchant
12. Curious Jane
13. Jenny and the Showman
14. Little Fan
15. Broken Window
16. Letty Young
17. Matty and Tom
18. The Orphans
19. John Madge
20. Philip Reeve
21. Henry Harris
22. £1 and £10,000
23. Brave Little Tom
24. Ella's Rose-bud
25. The Pedlar's Loan
26. Milly's New Year
27. Only a Ladybird
28. The First False Step
29. Richard Shaw

Charley's Disappointment; or, Making the Best of it. By Mrs. Carey Brock. 3d.

A Lad with a Good Character. 1d.

Orphan Boy; or, How Little John was Reclaimed. 1d.

Son of My Friend. 1d.

Juvenile Library. Small Books containing Stories for Children. Well illustrated. Nos. 1 to 72. One halfpenny each; and may also be had in assorted Sixpenny Packets, A, B, C, D, E, and F.

1. Fear of Ridicule
2. The Two Nests
3. Little Helpers
4. Anecdotes of Dogs
5. The Two Bears
6. Questions with Answers
7. Beautiful Garment
8. The Bird's Nest
9. The Organ Boy
10. Lessons on Kindness
11. Spring Flowers
12. True Duncan
13. Bread cast upon the Waters
14. Greek Testament
15. Brave Sailor Boy
16. "You Can't Straighten It."
17. Child Colporteur
18. Boy that could be trusted
19. The Golden Star
20. What a Blind Child can Do
21. Be Truthful
22. Child's Resolution
23. Soldier and Princess
24. Have you a Winter Garden
25. Trembling Eyelid
26. Willie Harris
27. The "Cry" Boy
28. Troublesome Joe
29. The Tell-Tale
30. John Reynolds
31. Pleasures of the Country
32. Bennie Wilson's Anti-Society
33. Robert, the Stone-Thrower
34. Little Frank and Old "Dobbin"
35. True Bravery
36. Nellie Lindsay
37. A Youthful Hero
38. The Clever Boy
39. Little Hugh's Tool-Box
40. Try Company
41. Remarkable Answer to Prayer
42. What Echo said
43. Girl at the Well
44. Juvenile Inquiries
45. The Young Cadet
46. Elijah in the Desert
47. Greedy Bill
48. A Happy New Year
49. "Please, Sir"
50. Young Sailor
51. Horses from the Wood
52. Little Bertha
53. White Feather of Peace
54. Helping Father to Garden
55. Indian Chief
56. Christmas Tree
57. It Rains
58. Young Patriot
59. "With a will, Joe"
60. Letter to Little Boys and Girls
61. Young Drummer's Patchwork Quilt
62. Poor Boy who became a great Painter
63. Little Gleaner
64. Pincher's Friend
65. Help a Fellow-Creature
66. Bargain with the Pump
67. Bridal Wine-cup
68. Plymouth Boatman
69. True and False Courage
70. Be Kind to your Mother
71. What the Birds say
72. Ministry of Flowers

BOOKS FOR GIRLS.

The Babes in the Basket; or, Daph and her Charge. Cloth, 2s. 6d.

The Church Mouse. By Mrs. H. J. Burge Smith. A Story of a Little Girl and Mouse. 1s.

"Come Home, Mother!" A Story for Mothers. By Nelsie Brook. Cloth, 1s.

Cousin Bessie: A Story of Youthful Earnestness. Cloth, 1s.

Crosses of Childhood; or, Little Alice and her Friend. Cloth, 1s.

The Governess; or, The Missing Pencil Case. Cloth, 1s.

Jenny's Geranium; or, The Prize Flower of a London Court. Cloth, 1s.

Jessie Dyson. A Tale for the Young. By John A. Walker. With numerous illustrations. Cloth, 1s.

Lucy Bell's First Place. A Story for Domestics. Cloth, 1s.

Marie and the Seven Children. A Tale for Elder Girls. By Mrs. Geldart. Cloth, 1s.

Maude's Visit to Sandy Beach. By the Author of "Crosses of Childhood." Cloth, 1s.

Mind whom you Marry; or, The Gardener's Daughter. By the Rev. C. G. Rowe. Cloth, 1s.

Mother's Stories for her Children. By Mrs. Carus Wilson. Cloth, 1s.

Rachel; or, Little Faults. By Charlotte Elizabeth. Cloth, 1s.

Rosa; or, The Two Castles. By Miss Bradburn. Cloth, 1s.

Sybil and Her Live Snowball. By the Author of "Dick and his Donkey." 1s.

Nettie Leigh's Birthday. By A. E. R. Cloth, 6d.

Procrastinating Mary. A Story for Young Girls. 6d.

Rosa May's Christmas Dream, and What Came of it. 6d.

The Tiny Library. See "Books for Boys."

Tottie's Christmas Shoes. By Nelsie Brook. Cover printed in colours, 6d.

Annie Baker; or, The Lit- tle Pilgrim. By Margaret Murchison. 3d.

Faithful Bessie. By the Author of "Dick and his Donkey." 3d.

More Ways than One; or, The Little Missionary. By Mrs. Carey Brock. 3d.

What Small Hands may do; or, Filial Affection. 3d.

Young Susan's First Place; or, A Young Servant's Difficulties. 3d.

A Little Voice. A Sudden Snare. By Mrs. C. L. Balfour. 1d.

On Dress. By the Rev. John Wesley. 1d.

FOR KITCHEN LIBRARIES.

(See also Temperance, and Sunday Schools.)

The Dairyman's Daugh- ter: an Authentic Narrative. By the Rev. Legh Richmond, M.A. Cloth, 1s. 6d.; gilt, 2s. 6d.

Good Servants, Good Wives, and Happy Homes. By the Rev. T. H. Walker. Cloth, 1s. 6d.

The History of Susan Gray, as related by a Clergyman. By Mrs. Sherwood. Cloth, 1s. 6d.

Nancy Wimble, the Vil- lage Gossip. Cloth, 1s. 6d.

Nurse Ellerton: A Tale of Domestic Life. By the Author of "Jenny's Geranium." Cloth, 1s. 6d.

Servant's Magazine. The Three Volumes for the years 1867 to 1869. Cloth, 1s. 6d.; gilt edges, 2s.

Waste not, Want not: a Book for Servants. Cloth, 1s. 6d.

Bible Pattern of a Good Woman. By Mrs. Balfour. Cloth, 1s.

Cliff Hut; or, The Perils of a Fisherman's Family. Cloth, 1s.

Homely Hints on House- hold Management. By Mrs. C. L. Balfour. Cloth, 1s.

Lucy Bell's First Place. A Story for Domestics. By Nelsie Brook. Cloth, 1s.

Mind whom you Marry; or, The Gardener's Daughter. By the Rev. C. G. Rowe. Cloth, 1s.

Toil and Trust; or, Life- Story of Patty, the Workhouse Girl. By Mrs. Balfour. Cloth, 1s.

Widow Green and her Three Nieces. By Mrs. Ellis. Cloth, 1s.

Hannah Twist: a Story about Temper. By Miss Bakewell. Cloth, 6d.

Kitchen Temperance Society, and how it was Formed. Cloth, 6d.

Scrub; or, The Workhouse Boy's First Start in Life. Cloth, 6d.

The Victim; or, An Evening's Amusement at the "Vulture." Cloth, 6d.

Address to Young Servants, especially to those just entering Service. 3d.

Faithful Bessie. By the Author of "Dick and his Donkey." 3d.

Message from Whitechapel; or, Scenes in a London Hospital By Augustus Johnstone. 3d.

Uncle David's Advice to Young Men and Young Women on Marriage. 3d.

Uncle David's Visit to a New Married Wife, and the Counsels he gave her. 3d.

Young Susan's First Place; or, A Young Servant's Difficulties. 3d.

"It's Nobbut" and "Niver Heed." By Robert Baker, Esq., Inspector of Factories. 2d.

Aunt Mary's Preserving Kettle. By T. S. Arthur. 1d.

FOR THE NURSERY, &C.

The Mother's Picture Alphabet. A Page to each Letter. Dedicated by the Queen's special permission to H.R.H. Princess Beatrice. Paper Boards, 5s.

Little Rosebud's Album. With 130 Illustrations by Sir John Gilbert, Harrison Weir, Robert Barnes, etc. Being a Companion Volume to "My Pet's Album." Cloth, 5s.

My Darling's Album. A companion volume to "My Pet's Album," with full-page illustrations. Cloth, 5s.

My Mother. By Ann Taylor. A Series of Twelve Oil Pictures, to illustrate this well-known ballad. Cloth, gilt, 5s.

My Pet's Album. A Book for the Nursery. Cloth, 5s.

My Pet's Picture Book. With full-page illustrations. Cloth, 5s. Companion vol. to "My Pet's Album."

Child-land. Full of Pictures and suitable letterpress. Cloth, 4s.

The Children's Picture Roll. Consisting of 31 Illustrated Leaves, with large type letterpress, suitable to hang up in the Nursery, Schoolroom, etc. Price 3s.

Natural History Picture Roll, consisting of 31 Illustrated Leaves, with simple large type letterpress, suitable to hang up in the Nursery, Schoolroom, etc. Price 3s.

The Babes in the Basket; or, Daph and her Charge Cloth, 2s. 6d.

Music for the Nursery. Revised by Philip Phillips, the "Singing Pilgrim" A Collection of Fifty of the Sweet Pieces for the "Little Ones" that have appeared in the "Infant's Magazine," etc. Handsomely bound in cloth, 2s. 6d.

Songs and Hymns for the Little Ones. Compiled by Uncle John. With numerous Engravings, new edition. Cloth, 2s. 6d.

Important Truths in Simple Verse. Cloth, 1s. 6d.

Kitty King. A Book for the Nursery. With full-page engravings. Cloth, 1s. 6d.

Rhymes worth Remembering. Cloth, 1s.

The "Children's Friend" Series. Coloured covers, and many engravings. 1s. each.
  1. Talk with the Little Ones
  2. Ronald's Reason; or, The Little Cripple
  3. Sybil and her Live Snowball
  4. Short Steps for Little Feet

5. How Peter's Pound became a Penny
6. How Paul's Penny became a Pound
7. John Oriel's First Start in Life
8. Dick and his Donkey
9. The Young Potato-Roasters
10. Little Woodman and his Dog Cæsar
11. The Church Mouse
12. Herbert's First Year at Bramford
13. Buster and Baby Jim
14. Grumbling Tommy and Contented Harry
15. The Bird's Nest.

The above books, printed in large type, form an attractive little library for the young folks.

The New Illustrated Primer. By Old Humphrey. Revised by T. B. S. In large type. Cloth, 1s.; paper covers, 6d. This copiously illustrated Primer will, it is hoped, be found a little treasure in the nursery.

The Tiny Library. Books printed in large type. Nos. 1 to 29. Cloth, 6d. each.

Little Tracts for Little Folks. By various authors. In packets 6d. Vol. 9d.

The Carol Singers. By Miss Matthews. 1d.

Juvenile Library. Small Books containing Stories for Children. Well Illustrated. Nos. 1 to 72. One halfpenny each, and may be had in assorted Sixpenny Packets—A, B, and C, D, E, and F.

THE SABBATH, ETC.

The Christian Monitor; or, Selections from Pious Authors. Cloth, 2s. 6d.; cloth, gilt edges, 3s. 6d.

Illustrated Sabbath Facts; or, God's Weekly Gift to the Weary. Reprinted from the "British Workman." Cloth, 1s. 6d.

The Belief. Printed in Colours on Cartridge Paper. 22 by 15. 4d.

The Lord's Prayer. Printed in Colours on Cartridge Paper. 22 by 15. 4d.

Cabman's Holiday. By Miss Sinclair. 3d.

Farmer Ellicot; or, Begin and End with God. 3d.

Is Half better than the Whole? A Conversation about Sunday Trading. 1d.

Scripture Texts. Texts in Ornamental Borders. 1d.

Nellie Lindsay. ½d.

AGAINST SMOKING.

What Put my Pipe Out; or, Incidents in the Life of a Clergyman. Cloth, 1s.

How Sam Adam's Pipe became a Pig. By J. W. Kirton, Author of "Buy your own Cherries." 6d.

Hints for Smokers, and on the Use and Abuse of Tobacco. 3d.

What's that to me? Number of the Illustrated Wall Papers. 1d.

MISCELLANEOUS.

Gleanings for the Drawing-room. In Prose and Verse. Compiled by T. B. S. Medallion on side, cloth, gilt edges, 10s. 6d.

Half - hours with the Kings and Queens of England, containing short sketches by W. H. G. Kingston, and portraits drawn by Edward Hughes, from the best authorities in the British Museum, of each monarch. Cloth, gilt edges, 10s. 6d.

Happy Half-hours. Being Ten Readings for Working Men. Bound up in one volume. By various Authors. Cloth, 3s.

Children's Friend in Arabic. Translated by Rev. A. Tien, M.A. Cloth, gilt edges, 2s. 6d.

Four Sermons. By the Rev. John Wesley. Cloth, plain, 6d.

The Rod and its Uses; or, Thomas Dodd and Bill Collins. By Author of "My Flowers." Cloth, 6d.

Voice of Childhood; or,
The Influence and Poetry, the Wrongs and the Wants of our Little Ones. By John De Fraine. Cloth, 6d.

Readings for the Drawing
Room and Lecture Hall. Well printed, with cover, price 4d.
- No. 1. The Learned Jew.
- ,, 2. Dan, the Boy Bishop.

Two Irish Scenes. 3d.

Captain Ball's Experience. 1d.

Chimney Sweepers and
their Friends. By R. P. Scott. 1d.

The Cure of Evil Speaking. By Rev. John Wesley. 1d.

Election Papers. 16 pp.
Tracts written by various Authors. 1d. each.
1. Don't Sell your Birthright
2. Ned Biddle's Teasers
3. How shall you Vote?
4. I'll Vote for You
5. Honest Voter

"God Save the Green."
A few words to the Irish People. By Mrs. S. C. Hall. 2d.

Going Home for Christmas. 1d.

How to Grow a Plant
and Win a Prize. 1d.

On the Use of Money.
By Rev. John Wesley. 1d.

On Redeeming the Time.
By Rev. John Wesley. 1d.

Sam Adams, Welch. 1d.

Halfpenny Illustrated
Books. 32mo. An assorted packet may be had, containing one of each of Nos. 1 to 24, price 1s.

Juvenile Pictorial Gallery.
This Series of handsome Illustrated Sheets for the Walls of Schools, Nurseries, &c., is specially commended to the notice of Parents, Schoolmasters, and Teachers.
1. Old Age and Childhood
2. The Little Wren
3. Careless Tom Jenkins
4. Horses from the Wood
5. The Power of Prayer
6. The Honest Savoyard
7. Daniel and his Friends
8. "I Will Fight!"
9. Hot Coals; or, How Fritz was conquered
10. Hole in the Pocket
11. Hazel Dell
12. The Child Samuel
13. Celebrated Blacksmiths
14. Elijah and the Ravens
15. The Zebra
16. The Cow and Calf
17. The Goose
18. The Soldier Boy's Quilt
19. The Early Riser
20. Duck and Ducklings
21. The Yak
22. War and Want
23. Italian Peasant Boy
24. The Sloth
25. The Peacock
26. The Nightingale
27. The Quail

Nos. 1 to 24 of these Sheets of the Juvenile Pictorial Gallery may be had in two packets, A and B, containing 12 numbers in each, price one shilling. May be ordered through any bookseller. A Specimen Number sent post free in exchange for two penny stamps by S. W. Partridge and Co., 9, Paternoster-row, London.

Five Shilling Packets of
Back Numbers of any of the following Illustrated Periodicals may be had as under, being less than half-price:—

British Workman Packet, containing 125 copies, 5s.

Children's Friend Packet, containing 125 copies, 5s.

Friendly Visitor Packet, containing 125 copies, 5s.

Band of Hope Review Packet, containing 250 copies, 5s.

Infant's Magazine Packet, containing 125 copies, 5s.

Family Friend Packet, containing 125 copies, 5s.

The above charges do not include the cost of carriage, and only refer to Back Nos. Please be careful to order "Back Nos. Packets."

Illustrated Fly-Leaves.
Four-page Reprints from the "Friendly Visitor," "British Workman," &c. Specially commended to Tract Distributors, Sunday School Teachers, &c.
1. Providence will Provide
2. Poor Joseph
3. A Remarkable Contrast
4. Doing things on a Large Scale
5. Patched Window
6. A Thoughtful Wife
7. Daily Teachings
8. A Crown or, Does it Pay?
9. Railway Guard
10. Old Uncle Johnson
11. The Debt is paid
12. Please, Sir, will you Read it?
13. Please, Father, Come Home Early
14. Rees Pritchard and the Goat
15. The Beaten Carpet

16. Blue Cart with the Red Wheels
17. Secret of England's Greatness
18. Uncle Anthony
19. Blind Mary
20. Niff and his Dogs
21. The Singing Cobbler of Hamburg
22. Hunter's Home, &c.
23. That Great Fountain
24. Losses by Religion
25. Officer and the Verse on the Wall
26. What's This?
27. The Infidel Officer
28. The Singing Carpenter
29. Alone with God
30. Old Sailor and the Bible Reader
31. A Lady and the Card Players
32. The Windmill's Defect
33. The Singing Pilgrim
34. Thomas Brown
35. Five "Wadmen" in Workhouse
36. "There, you've gone over it!"
37. "Father, don't go"
38. "Hold! Fire if you dare!"
39. The Great Spirit
40. The Weekly Day of Rest
41. Sailor's Funeral
42. Aunt Bessy's Proverb
43. Auction at Sea.
44. Gooseberry Basket
45. Sea-boy's Story
46. Sunday Morning's Dream
47. Jack and the Yellow Boys
48. Albatross and the Soldier
49. Turning Point
50. Scripture Patchwork Quilt
51. Dark Without, Light Within
52. Michael Donovan
53. Old Deist
54. Dr. Ely and the Old Negress
55. How can these things be?
56. Blind Cobbler
57. The Reprieve
58. A Little Child shall Lead Them
59. Wilt Thou Use or Abuse thy Trust?
60. No Swearing Allowed
61. The Soldier in the Cell
62. A Prodigal's Return
63. "Does you love God?"
64. Jim Lineham's Happy Blunder
65. Mr. Collins and the Smoker
66. Yeddie's First and Last Communion
67. Meeting of Chimney Sweepers
68. How John Ross began to Kneel Down
69. A Life for a Life
70. Pull out the Staple!
71. A Happy Change; or, Good for Trade
72. John Brown, the Sensible Grave digger
73. Twopence a Day, and what it accomplished
74. A Gentle Reproof
75. "Will Father be a Goat, Mother?"
76. The Collier's Widow
77. Lost! Lost!
78. The Five Steps
79. The Door in the Heart
80. The Richest Man in the Parish
81. A Prodigal Restored
82. The Lost Sheep
83. John Morton's New Harmonium
84. Losings' Bank and Savings' Bank
85. Buy your own Cherries
86. Harry's Pint; or, Threepence a Day
87. A Plea for the Birds
88. The False Pilot and the True One
89. Swallowing a Yard of Land
90. Sceptic and Welsh Girl
91. The Logic of Life
92. The Life Preserver.
93. The Lawyer's Son; or, The Changed Family
94. The Plunge into the River
95. The Sceptic and the Minister
96. "I will Knock Again"
97. Ned Stokes, the Man-o'-War's-Man
98. The Two Gardeners
99. The Weaver's Lamp
100. The French Nobleman and Physician

These Illustrated Fly-Leaves may be had through any bookseller, or from 9, Paternoster-row, London, at the rate of 2s. 6d. per 100; or in shilling packets, in two volumes, cloth, 1s. 6d. each; gilt edges, 2s. 6d., containing 40 assorted numbers in each, and complete vol. 1 to 100, cloth plain, 4s. 6d.; gilt edges, 6s.

Portraits with Broad

Margins, suitable for framing. Printed on toned paper, 6d. each
1. Abraham Lincoln
2. Princess of Wales and Infant Prince
3. Richard Cobden. By Henry Anelay
4. The Queen. A Medallion Portrait of Her Majesty, with a facsimile of her Autograph
5. Prince Albert. A Medallion of the late Prince
6. Prince and Princess of Wales
7. Garibaldi. Coloured Portrait. From a Photograph by Negretti and Zambra
8. Lord Brougham
9. Napoleon III.
10. Princess Louise and Marquis of Lorne. 1d.

ALMANACS.

Animals' Friend Almanac. With costly Engravings and Letterpress. 1d.

Band of Hope Almanac. With costly Engravings and Letterpress. 1d.

British Workman Almanac. With costly Engravings and Letterpress. 1d.

Everyone's Almanac. 16 pages 4to. With numerous Engravings. 1d.

FOREIGN PUBLICATIONS.

Foreign "British Workman."
Printed in the following languages. 1d. each number.

Malagasy	No. 1
German	" 1—2
Dutch	" 1
Spanish	Nos. 1—15
Italian	" 1—4
French	" 1—12
Polish	" 1—3
Norwegian	" 1—2
Portuguese	" 1
Russian	" 1

Spanish, Vol. 1, coloured cover, 1s. 6d.

French "Children's Friend."
Nos. 1 to 8. 1d. each number.

Foreign "Infant's Magazine."
Printed in various languages. 1d. each number.

German	No. 1—2
French	" 1—8
Italian	" 1
Spanish	" 1—8

Foreign Illustrated Fly Leaves.

Spanish	Nos. 1 to 8.	2s. 6d. per 100
Italian	" 1 to 8.	2s. 6d. per 100
French	" 1 to 4.	2s. 6d. per 100
Welsh	" 1 to 4.	2s. 6d. per 100

Foreign Illustrated Wall Papers.
Printed in the following languages. 1d. each

Malagasy	Nos. 1
Maori	" 1
Italian	" 1—2—4
Welsh	" 1—2
Spanish	" 1—2
Persian	" 1
Chinese	" 1—3
Hawaiian	" 1
French	" 1—8
Fijian	" 1—2
Turkish	" 1
Urdu	" 1—2
Tamil	" 1—2
Hindi	" 1—2

Foreign Almanacs. 1d. each.
Italian Almanac. With costly Illustrations.
Spanish Almanac. With costly Illustrations.

Spanish Primer.
Well Illustrated. Intended to be used as a Lesson Book in Spanish Schools. 1s.

Jacobi Ben Israel, the Learned Jew.
In Hebrew. Paper cover and gilt edges.

Bought with a Price.
In French. 2d.

PERIODICALS.

One Penny Monthly, Fourpence Quarterly. New Series.

The Family Friend.
Vol. for 1875. Covers printed in colours, 1s. 6d.; Cloth, 2s.; Gilt, 2s. 6d. each. Illustrated by First-Class Artists. With Narratives and Articles for Fathers, Mothers, Children, and Servants. A piece of Music, suitable for the Family or the Nursery in each number. Printed on toned paper. Volumes for 1872 to 1874 still on sale.

In Numbers, Monthly, price One Penny.

British Workman.
With Full-page Pictures. The Yearly Part for 1875, with cover, printed in colours, price 1s. 6d. Cloth, Gilt Edges, 2s. 6d. Many of the Yearly Parts are at present kept on sale.
The Five-year Volumes (1865-69; 70-74;) Cloth, 9s.; Gilt Edges, 10s. 6d. each.

In Numbers, Monthly, price One Penny.

Children's Friend.
With Full-page Pictures. The Yearly Volume for 1875, with cover printed in colours, price 1s. 6d.; Cloth, 2s.; Gilt Edges, 2s. 6d. each. A piece of Music suitable for Children appears in each number.
Volumes 1862 to 1874 are at present kept on sale, in three sorts of binding, as above.

In Numbers, Monthly, price One Penny.

Infant's Magazine.
With Full-page Pictures. The Yearly Volume for 1875, with cover printed in colours, 1s. 6d.; Cloth, 2s.; Gilt Edges, 2s. 6d. A piece of Music appears in each number.
The Volumes from 1867 kept on sale, in three sorts of binding, as above.

In Numbers, Monthly, Price One Penny.

The Friendly Visitor.
Illustrated. A Magazine for the Aged. Printed in bold Type. The Yearly Volume for 1875, coloured cover, 1s. 6d.; Cloth, 2s.; Gilt Edges, 2s. 6d.
Volumes from 1867 in three sorts of binding, as above.

In Numbers, Monthly, One Halfpenny.

Band of Hope Review.
With Full-page Pictures. The Yearly Part for 1875, with cover printed in colours, price 1s.; Cloth, Gilt Edges, 2s. Complete Edition (1851-70), in Two Volumes, Cloth, 10s.; Gilt Edges, 12s. each. The Second Series (1861-75), in Three Volumes, Cloth 5s.; Gilt, 6s. each. All the Yearly Parts from the commencement (1851) are at present on sale.

RECENT ISSUES.

Half-hours with the Kings and Queens of England, containing Short Sketches by W. H. G. Kingston, and Portraits drawn by Edward Hughes, from the best authorities in the British Museum, of each Monarch. Gilt edges, 10s. 6d.

Our Zoological Friends; or, Conversations of an Uncle with his Nephews and Nieces about Animals, &c. By Harland Coultas. Cloth, 6s.

My Darling's Album. A companion volume to "My Pet's Album." With Full-page Illustrations. Cloth, 5s.

Natural History Picture-Roll, consisting of Thirty-one Illustrated Leaves on Natural History Subjects, with simple Large Type Letterpress. Suitable to hang up in the Nursery, Schoolroom, &c. Price 3s.

The Best Things. By the Rev. Dr. Newton. With numerous Illustrations. Cloth, 2s. 6d.

The King's Highway. By the Rev. Dr. Newton. With numerous Illustrations. Cloth, 2s. 6d.

Vignettes of American History. By Mary Howitt. New Edition, with Full-page Engravings. Cloth, 1s. 6d.

A Mother's Stories for her Children. By the late Mrs. Carus Wilson. New Edition. Cloth, 1s.

Digging a Grave with a Wine-glass. By Mrs. S. C. Hall. New Edition, with Engravings. Cloth, 1s.

Poor Blossom; the Story of a Horse. Respectfully dedicated to the Royal Society for the Prevention of Cruelty to Animals. Cloth, 1s.

Anecdotes of Animals, etc. 1d. each.
   No. 5. Blackbird's Nest.
    ,, 6. How to manage Horses.

El Obrero. No. 15. 1d.

Does it Answer? a Tract for Soldiers and Sailors. 1d.

Illustrated Penny Read-ings. 1d. each.
   No. 37. Woman's Crusade.

Illustrated Wall-bills. 1d. each.
   No. 76. The Well-to-do Cabman
    ,, 77. The Costermonger.

Friends of the Friendless. By Mrs. C. L. Balfour. New Edition, Cloth 6d.

Juvenile Library. Packet F., 6d. In Numbers, Halfpenny each.

No Work, No Bread. By the Author of "Jessica's First Prayer." Cloth, 6d.

The Pearly Gates. By Mrs. C. Rigg, Author of "Lost in the Snow." A Book for Sunday-school Children. Cloth, 6d.

Readings for the Draw-ing-Room and Lecture-Hall. Well printed on toned paper, 4to size, with cover. Price 4d. each.
   No. 1. The Learned Jew.
    ,, 2. Dan, the Boy Bishop, etc

British Workman Series of Tracts. With Cover and Engravings, 2d. each.
   No. 9. He Drinks.
    ,, 10. Doing His Duty.
    ,, 11. Good Fruit.
    ,, 12. The Bent Shilling.
    ,, 13. The Drummer Boy.
    ,, 14. The Inch Augur.
    ,, 15. Split Navvy.
    ,, 16. "Put on the Break, Jim!"
    ,, 17. Taking up of Barney O'Rourke.
    ,, 18. The House that John Built.
    ,, 19. Articles of War.
    ,, 20. Little Sam Groves.

Coloured Series. With Coloured Covers and Engravings. 2d. each.
   No. 20. "Not a Drop more, Daniel."
    ,, 21. Mike Slattery.
    ,, 22. The Holly Boy.
    ,, 23. Melodious Mat.

New Envelope Series of Tracts, for enclosure in Letters. Halfpenny each.
   No. 1. "That's thee, Jem!"
    ,, 2. The Richest Man in the Parish.
    ,, 3. The Secret of England's Greatness.
    ,, 4. "The Debt is Paid."

LONDON: S. W. PARTRIDGE & CO., 9, PATERNOSTER ROW.

www.ingramcontent.com/pod-product-compliance
Lightning Source LLC
Chambersburg PA
CBHW080437110426
42743CB00016B/3188